Real Stories of Nuclear Tragedies

Shah Rukh

Published by Shah Rukh, 2024.

While every precaution has been taken in the preparation of this book, the publisher assumes no responsibility for errors or omissions, or for damages resulting from the use of the information contained herein.

REAL STORIES OF NUCLEAR TRAGEDIES

First edition. May 10, 2024.

Copyright © 2024 Shah Rukh.

ISBN: 979-8224160273

Written by Shah Rukh.

Table of Contents

Prologue

The discovery of nuclear energy marked a turning point in human history, a gateway to boundless power and potential. What began as a theoretical exploration of atomic particles quickly transformed into one of the most powerful—and dangerous—forces known to humanity. The promise of nuclear energy brought with it dreams of limitless electricity, advanced medical treatments, and even peace through deterrence. But it also unleashed a darker reality—a world shadowed by the threat of catastrophic accidents, contamination, and devastating loss.

This book, *Real Stories of Nuclear Tragedies*, delves into the complex history of nuclear incidents across the globe. From the well-known disasters of Chernobyl and Fukushima to the lesser-known but equally harrowing events like the Goiania accident in Brazil and the SL-1 reactor meltdown in Idaho, each chapter uncovers the human stories behind these tragedies. The consequences of nuclear energy and weapons are felt far beyond the blast radius or the reactor walls. They ripple through communities, alter ecosystems, and leave a legacy of fear, suffering, and resilience.

The chapters that follow chronicle not only the technical details of these incidents but also the lives forever changed by them. We explore the bravery of those who risked their lives to contain radioactive leaks, the scientists who struggled to understand and mitigate the damage, and the ordinary citizens caught in the fallout—both literal and figurative. We also examine the political, social, and ethical dilemmas that these nuclear incidents have sparked and how they continue to shape policy and public opinion today.

Nuclear energy and technology remain a controversial topic, one that balances precariously between promise and peril. As we journey through these real stories of nuclear tragedies, we gain a deeper understanding of the delicate dance between harnessing atomic power and managing its inherent dangers. We confront the haunting question: is the potential benefit worth the inevitable risk?

This book serves as both a historical record and a cautionary tale, reminding us that with great power comes great responsibility. It is an invitation to reflect on the lessons learned from the past and consider the choices we make for the future. Join us as we navigate the hazardous terrain of nuclear energy's dark side, bearing witness to the enduring impact of its tragic chapters on the world stage.

Chapter 1: Three Mile Island Accident

The Three Mile Island accident, which occurred on March 28, 1979, is widely regarded as the most serious accident in the history of the American commercial nuclear power generating industry. This incident, which took place at the Three Mile Island Nuclear Generating Station in Pennsylvania, shook public confidence in nuclear energy and had far-reaching implications for the future of nuclear power in the United States and around the world. Although the event ultimately resulted in only a small release of radioactive gases and no immediate injuries or fatalities, its impact on the perception of nuclear safety and the nuclear power industry was profound. This detailed examination of the Three Mile Island accident will explore the technical, operational, and regulatory aspects of the event, as well as its lasting effects on the nuclear industry and public policy.

The Three Mile Island Nuclear Generating Station: Background and Design

The Three Mile Island Nuclear Generating Station, located on a small island in the Susquehanna River near Harrisburg, Pennsylvania, was a state-of-the-art facility for its time. The plant consisted of two pressurized water reactors (PWRs): Unit 1, which began operation in 1974, and Unit 2, which came online in December 1978. The reactors were designed and constructed by Babcock & Wilcox, a leading engineering company with significant experience in nuclear technology. The plant's design featured several safety systems intended to prevent or mitigate accidents, including multiple layers of physical barriers and redundant cooling systems.

Unit 2, the reactor involved in the accident, was rated at 906 megawatts of electrical power and employed a sophisticated system of pumps, pipes, and valves to circulate coolant and remove heat from the reactor core. The core itself contained thousands of fuel rods, each filled with uranium dioxide pellets, which underwent fission to produce heat. The heat generated by the fission process was used to convert water into steam, which then drove turbines to generate electricity.

The Accident: A Sequence of Failures

The Three Mile Island accident began in the early hours of March 28, 1979, when a series of mechanical failures and operator errors led to a partial meltdown of the reactor core in Unit 2. The chain of events that culminated in the accident was set in motion by a relatively minor problem: the failure of a feedwater pump, which was responsible for supplying water to the steam generators. This failure initiated a shutdown of the main feedwater system, triggering an automatic reactor shutdown, or "scram," designed to halt the nuclear fission process by inserting control rods into the reactor core.

However, the shutdown of the feedwater system also caused a rapid increase in pressure within the reactor's primary cooling system. To relieve this pressure, a pilot-operated relief valve (PORV) was designed to open and release steam into a pressurizer. Unfortunately, the PORV became stuck open after relieving the pressure, allowing coolant to escape from the reactor core. Despite this, control room operators were unaware that the valve was stuck open because the indicator light on their control panels erroneously showed that the valve was closed.

As coolant continued to leak from the reactor core, the water level in the core dropped, exposing the fuel rods. The exposed rods began to overheat, and the zirconium cladding surrounding the fuel pellets reacted with steam to produce hydrogen gas. The buildup of hydrogen created the risk of a hydrogen explosion, which could have further compromised the integrity of the reactor vessel.

Compounding the situation was the fact that the control room operators misinterpreted the signals they were receiving from their instruments. Believing that the reactor was still adequately cooled, they reduced the flow of emergency cooling water to the reactor, exacerbating the loss of coolant and allowing the core to overheat further. By the time the operators realized the severity of the situation, a significant portion of the reactor core had already melted.

Immediate Response and Containment Efforts

The initial response to the accident was chaotic and marked by confusion both within the plant and among regulatory authorities. The plant's emergency systems eventually succeeded in reestablishing cooling to the reactor core, but by that time, approximately half of the core had melted. Despite the severity of the core damage, the containment building surrounding the reactor largely succeeded in preventing the release of most radioactive materials.

However, small amounts of radioactive gases, including xenon and krypton, were released into the environment over the course of several days. These releases prompted concern among the public and led to conflicting statements from government officials and the plant's operators about the potential health risks. The lack of clear and accurate information fueled public fear and speculation, leading to widespread panic in the surrounding communities.

Governor Richard Thornburgh of Pennsylvania faced intense pressure to take decisive action. On March 30, two days after the accident began, he ordered the evacuation of pregnant women and young children within a five-mile radius of the plant. This precautionary measure, while not based on any immediate threat, reflected the growing anxiety and uncertainty surrounding the situation.

The Role of the Nuclear Regulatory Commission (NRC)

The Nuclear Regulatory Commission (NRC), the federal agency responsible for overseeing the safety of nuclear power plants, played a crucial role in the response to the Three Mile Island accident. In the immediate aftermath of the incident, NRC officials worked around the clock to assess the situation, coordinate with plant operators, and communicate with the public.

The NRC dispatched a team of experts to the site to monitor the reactor's condition and provide guidance on containment and cleanup efforts. The commission also conducted a thorough investigation into the causes of the accident, leading to a series of regulatory reforms aimed at improving the safety and reliability of nuclear power plants.

One of the most significant outcomes of the NRC's investigation was the recognition that human error, rather than equipment failure alone, was a major factor in the accident. The commission's findings highlighted the need for better training for reactor operators, improved instrumentation, and more rigorous safety protocols. These recommendations led to widespread changes in the nuclear industry, including the development of more advanced control room simulators for operator training and the implementation of more stringent safety standards.

Public Reaction and the Impact on Nuclear Power

The Three Mile Island accident had a profound impact on public opinion regarding nuclear power. Prior to the accident, there was broad support for the expansion of nuclear energy as a clean and efficient alternative to fossil fuels. However, the events at Three Mile Island shattered public confidence in the safety of nuclear power plants and led to widespread fear and opposition to nuclear energy.

The accident also had significant political ramifications. In the United States, the nuclear power industry faced intense scrutiny from lawmakers, environmental groups, and the public. The construction of new nuclear power plants slowed dramatically, and many planned projects were canceled altogether. The accident also spurred the creation of grassroots anti-nuclear movements, which organized protests, legal challenges, and public awareness campaigns against nuclear energy.

In the years following the accident, the nuclear power industry underwent a period of stagnation, with no new reactors ordered in the United States for several decades. The Three Mile Island accident became a symbol of the potential dangers of nuclear power and a rallying point for those opposed to its use.

Long-Term Consequences and Lessons Learned

The Three Mile Island accident had far-reaching consequences for the nuclear power industry, both in the United States and around the world. In the years following the accident, the NRC implemented a series of regulatory changes aimed at preventing similar incidents in the future. These changes included:

- **Improved Operator Training:** The NRC mandated more comprehensive training programs for reactor operators, including the use of full-scale simulators to practice emergency scenarios. This training emphasized the importance of recognizing and responding to abnormal conditions, as well as the need for clear communication and teamwork during emergencies.
- **Enhanced Safety Systems:** The NRC required the installation of additional safety systems and equipment at nuclear power plants to provide multiple layers of protection against accidents. These systems included more reliable pressure relief valves, improved instrumentation, and

additional emergency cooling capabilities.

- **Strengthened Regulatory Oversight:** The NRC increased its oversight of nuclear power plants, conducting more frequent inspections and requiring more detailed reporting of operational data. The commission also established stricter criteria for the licensing and operation of nuclear reactors.
- **Public Communication:** The Three Mile Island accident underscored the importance of clear and accurate communication with the public during nuclear emergencies. The NRC and the nuclear industry developed protocols for providing timely and transparent information to the public and the media in the event of an accident.

The lessons learned from the Three Mile Island accident contributed to significant improvements in nuclear safety and operational practices. However, the accident also had a lasting impact on the perception of nuclear power. Despite the technological and regulatory advances made in the aftermath of the accident, public skepticism and opposition to nuclear energy persisted, particularly in the United States.

The Cleanup and Decommissioning Process

The cleanup and decommissioning of the damaged reactor at Three Mile Island were a complex and costly process that took more than a decade to complete. The initial focus of the cleanup effort was on removing the damaged fuel from the reactor core and stabilizing the site to prevent any further release of radioactive materials.

In the years following the accident, specialized teams worked to remove the melted fuel, decontaminate the reactor building, and safely store the radioactive waste. The cleanup operation was closely monitored by the NRC and other regulatory agencies to ensure that all safety protocols were followed.

The final phase of the decommissioning process involved the permanent closure of the Unit 2 reactor and the dismantling of equipment and structures that were no longer needed. The entire cleanup and decommissioning effort cost an estimated $1 billion, a significant financial burden for the plant's operators and the nuclear industry.

Global Implications and the Future of Nuclear Power

The Three Mile Island accident had a global impact, prompting other countries to reevaluate their nuclear safety practices and regulatory frameworks. In some countries, the accident led to the adoption of more stringent safety standards and the development of new technologies to enhance reactor safety. In others, it fueled anti-nuclear sentiment and influenced energy policy decisions.

For example, in Western Europe, the accident contributed to a growing public movement against nuclear power, leading to the suspension or cancellation of nuclear projects in countries like Germany, Sweden, and Italy. In contrast, countries like France and Japan, which had significant investments in nuclear energy, responded by strengthening their safety regulations and continuing to expand their nuclear power programs.

The long-term legacy of the Three Mile Island accident is a complex one. While it undoubtedly contributed to the advancement of nuclear safety, it also cast a long shadow over the industry, shaping public perception and energy policy for decades. The accident remains a pivotal moment in the history of nuclear power, a reminder of the potential risks associated with nuclear energy and the importance of vigilance, transparency, and safety in its use.

Chapter 2: Fukushima Daiichi Disaster

The Fukushima Daiichi nuclear disaster, which began on March 11, 2011, is one of the most catastrophic nuclear accidents in history. Triggered by a massive earthquake and tsunami, the disaster led to severe reactor meltdowns, explosions, and the release of significant amounts of radioactive materials into the environment. The impact of the Fukushima disaster was felt globally, raising serious concerns about the safety of nuclear power and leading to profound changes in energy policy and nuclear regulation. This comprehensive analysis delves into the causes, events, and far-reaching consequences of the Fukushima Daiichi disaster, examining both the technical and human factors that contributed to the tragedy.

The Fukushima Daiichi Nuclear Power Plant: Design and Operation

The Fukushima Daiichi Nuclear Power Plant, operated by the Tokyo Electric Power Company (TEPCO), is located on the eastern coast of Japan in the Fukushima Prefecture. The plant, commissioned in the 1970s, consisted of six boiling water reactors (BWRs), a type of reactor commonly used worldwide. These reactors were designed by General Electric, with additional construction and maintenance carried out by Japanese companies.

Each reactor at the Fukushima Daiichi plant operated on the principle of boiling water to produce steam, which would then drive turbines to generate electricity. The reactors were housed within containment structures designed to prevent the release of radioactive materials in the event of an accident. The plant also included extensive cooling systems, which circulated water to remove heat from the reactor cores and spent fuel pools.

Despite the plant's design and safety measures, it was built in an area prone to earthquakes and tsunamis. While it was engineered to withstand significant seismic activity, the scale of the disaster that unfolded in 2011 exceeded the plant's safety margins.

The Great East Japan Earthquake and Tsunami: The Natural Disasters that Triggered the Crisis

On March 11, 2011, at 2:46 PM JST, a powerful undersea megathrust earthquake struck off the northeastern coast of Japan. Known as the Great East Japan Earthquake, or the Tōhoku earthquake, it registered a magnitude of 9.0 on the Richter scale, making it one of the most powerful earthquakes ever recorded. The earthquake's epicenter was approximately 130 kilometers east of the Oshika Peninsula, and it generated a massive tsunami with waves reaching heights of up to 40 meters.

The tsunami struck the Fukushima Daiichi Nuclear Power Plant with devastating force less than an hour after the earthquake. The plant's protective seawall, which was designed to withstand a tsunami of up to 5.7 meters, was overwhelmed by the much larger waves. The tsunami flooded the plant's lower levels, knocking out the electrical power supply and disabling the emergency diesel generators, which were essential for maintaining the cooling systems.

The Sequence of Events: From Earthquake to Meltdown

The disaster at Fukushima Daiichi unfolded rapidly in the hours and days following the earthquake and tsunami. The loss of power led to a cascading series of failures that ultimately resulted in the meltdown of three reactor cores and severe damage to a fourth reactor.

1. **Initial Impact and Loss of Power (March 11, 2011):**
    - The earthquake triggered an automatic shutdown, or

"scram," of the reactors at Fukushima Daiichi, halting the nuclear fission process. However, the decay heat generated by the reactors continued to require cooling.

- The tsunami flooded the plant, causing a complete station blackout by disabling both the external power grid and the emergency diesel generators. This loss of power left the plant without the ability to operate the cooling systems.

2. **Emergency Response and Cooling Failures:**

- With the cooling systems inoperable, the reactor cores began to overheat. TEPCO workers attempted to restore power and inject water into the reactors using alternative methods, including battery-powered pumps and fire engines, but these efforts were insufficient.

- As the water levels in the reactors dropped, the fuel rods became exposed, leading to overheating and the production of hydrogen gas through the zirconium-steam reaction. The buildup of hydrogen gas in the containment vessels created the risk of explosions.

3. **Hydrogen Explosions (March 12-15, 2011):**

- On March 12, a hydrogen explosion occurred in the reactor building of Unit 1, destroying the upper part of the building and releasing radioactive materials into the environment. Similar explosions occurred in Units 3 and 4 over the following days, further damaging the plant and releasing additional radioactive contamination.

- The explosions complicated efforts to control the situation, as they damaged critical infrastructure and created extremely hazardous conditions for the workers attempting to stabilize the reactors.

4. **Meltdown and Release of Radioactive Materials:**
    ○ Despite efforts to inject water into the reactors, the cores in Units 1, 2, and 3 experienced partial or complete meltdowns, where the fuel rods melted and accumulated at the bottom of the reactor vessels. In some cases, molten fuel is believed to have breached the reactor vessels and entered the containment structures.
    ○ Large quantities of radioactive materials, including iodine-131, cesium-137, and strontium-90, were released into the atmosphere, the ocean, and the surrounding environment. The release of radioactive materials was exacerbated by the venting of steam to reduce pressure within the reactors and the leaks caused by the explosions.

Evacuation and Immediate Impact on the Population

As the scale of the disaster became apparent, Japanese authorities ordered the evacuation of residents within a 20-kilometer radius of the Fukushima Daiichi plant. This evacuation zone was later expanded to 30 kilometers, affecting more than 150,000 people. The evacuation was chaotic, with many residents forced to leave their homes with little notice and uncertain when, or if, they would be able to return.

The release of radioactive materials raised concerns about acute and long-term health effects, particularly the risk of radiation-induced cancer. The Japanese government and international agencies, including the World Health Organization (WHO) and the International Atomic Energy Agency (IAEA), conducted extensive monitoring of radiation levels and provided guidance on protective measures, such as the distribution of iodine tablets to prevent the uptake of radioactive iodine by the thyroid gland.

The disaster also had significant psychological and social impacts on the affected population. The sudden displacement, fear of radiation exposure, and uncertainty about the future contributed to widespread anxiety, depression, and other mental health issues. The long-term disruption of communities and livelihoods further compounded the human toll of the disaster.

TEPCO's Response and the Role of the Japanese Government

TEPCO's response to the Fukushima disaster was widely criticized for its lack of preparedness, slow decision-making, and poor communication. In the immediate aftermath of the earthquake and tsunami, TEPCO struggled to assess the situation and implement effective measures to prevent the escalation of the crisis. The company's failure to anticipate and mitigate the risk of a station blackout, despite warnings from experts and previous incidents at other plants, was a significant factor in the severity of the disaster.

The Japanese government, led by Prime Minister Naoto Kan, faced immense pressure to manage the crisis and protect public safety. However, the government's response was also criticized for being slow, disorganized, and lacking transparency. Conflicting information from TEPCO, government agencies, and international experts contributed to confusion and distrust among the public.

One of the most controversial aspects of the government's response was its handling of information related to the spread of radioactive contamination. There were delays in disclosing the full extent of the radioactive releases, and the criteria for establishing evacuation zones were questioned by both domestic and international observers. The government's reluctance to issue mandatory evacuation orders in some highly contaminated areas also sparked criticism and legal challenges from affected residents.

International Response and Global Repercussions

The Fukushima disaster had profound implications for the global nuclear industry. The scale of the accident and the release of radioactive materials led to widespread concern about the safety of nuclear power plants, particularly those located in seismically active regions or coastal areas vulnerable to tsunamis.

In the immediate aftermath of the disaster, several countries took steps to review and, in some cases, phase out their nuclear energy programs. Germany, under Chancellor Angela Merkel, made the decision to accelerate the shutdown of its nuclear power plants, committing to a complete phase-out by 2022. Switzerland and Belgium also announced plans to gradually reduce their reliance on nuclear energy.

In other countries, the disaster prompted rigorous safety reviews of existing nuclear facilities and the implementation of new safety regulations. The IAEA and national nuclear regulators worldwide conducted assessments of nuclear power plants, focusing on their ability to withstand extreme natural events, such as earthquakes and tsunamis. These reviews led to the upgrading of safety features, such as the installation of additional backup power systems, enhanced flood protection measures, and improvements in emergency response protocols.

The Fukushima disaster also sparked debates about the future of nuclear energy as a low-carbon energy source in the context of global efforts to combat climate change. While some argued that the risks associated with nuclear power were too great, others contended that the lessons learned from Fukushima could lead to safer and more resilient nuclear technologies, which would play a critical role in reducing greenhouse gas emissions.

Long-Term Environmental and Health Consequences

The environmental impact of the Fukushima disaster has been significant and long-lasting. Large areas of land around the Fukushima Daiichi plant were contaminated with radioactive materials, leading to the creation of exclusion zones where human habitation is restricted. The decontamination of these areas has been a complex and costly process, involving the removal of contaminated soil, vegetation, and debris. Despite these efforts, some areas remain too contaminated for safe return, and the long-term ecological effects of the disaster are still being studied.

The release of radioactive materials into the ocean also raised concerns about the impact on marine life and the safety of seafood. Radioactive isotopes, such as cesium-137, were detected in seawater, sediments, and marine organisms far beyond the immediate vicinity of the plant. The Japanese government implemented strict monitoring and restrictions on fishing in the affected areas, but concerns about the long-term effects of radiation on the marine ecosystem persist.

In terms of health impacts, the most immediate concern was the potential for radiation exposure to cause cancer and other health problems in the affected population. However, studies conducted by the WHO and other organizations have found that, due to the prompt evacuation and other protective measures, the overall radiation doses received by the population were relatively low. While there is an increased risk of thyroid cancer among children exposed to radioactive iodine, the long-term health effects of the disaster are still being monitored.

The Decommissioning of Fukushima Daiichi: A Herculean Task

The decommissioning of the Fukushima Daiichi plant is a monumental challenge that is expected to take several decades and cost billions of dollars. The process involves the removal of the melted fuel debris from the damaged reactors, the safe disposal of radioactive waste, and the decontamination and dismantling of the plant's structures.

One of the most difficult tasks is the retrieval of the melted fuel, which is highly radioactive and poses significant risks to workers. TEPCO and the Japanese government have been working on developing advanced technologies, such as remotely operated robots and new containment methods, to safely carry out this work. The complexity of the decommissioning process has led to delays and cost overruns, and it is likely that the full decommissioning will not be completed until the second half of the 21st century.

In addition to the technical challenges, the decommissioning effort has faced social and legal obstacles. The ongoing storage and treatment of contaminated water, which has been used to cool the damaged reactors, is a contentious issue. The decision to gradually release treated water into the ocean, starting in 2023, has been met with opposition from local communities, environmental groups, and neighboring countries, particularly South Korea and China, who are concerned about the potential impact on the marine environment and fisheries.

Socio-Economic Impact: The Ripple Effect on Japan and Beyond

The Fukushima disaster had a profound socio-economic impact on Japan and the wider world. In Japan, the disaster led to a significant disruption of the energy supply, as the government ordered the shutdown of all nuclear power plants in the aftermath of the crisis. This decision resulted in a sharp increase in the country's reliance on fossil fuels, leading to higher energy costs, increased carbon emissions, and a greater vulnerability to global energy market fluctuations.

The economic impact of the disaster was also felt in the form of massive compensation and cleanup costs. TEPCO, which was effectively nationalized in the wake of the disaster, faced enormous financial liabilities, including compensation payments to affected residents, businesses, and farmers, as well as the costs associated with the decontamination and decommissioning efforts. The Japanese government also bore a significant financial burden, providing support for the affected communities and funding the long-term recovery efforts.

On a broader scale, the Fukushima disaster had implications for the global nuclear industry. The incident led to a decline in public confidence in nuclear power and increased scrutiny of nuclear safety standards. In some countries, this contributed to the cancellation or delay of planned nuclear projects, while in others, it prompted a renewed focus on alternative energy sources, such as renewables.

Legacy and Lessons Learned: Fukushima's Enduring Impact

The legacy of the Fukushima Daiichi disaster is one of profound lessons for the nuclear industry, policymakers, and society as a whole. The disaster highlighted the vulnerability of nuclear power plants to natural disasters, particularly in seismically active regions, and underscored the importance of robust safety measures, effective crisis management, and transparent communication.

One of the key lessons learned from Fukushima is the need for continuous improvement in nuclear safety. In the years following the disaster, nuclear regulators and operators worldwide have implemented significant enhancements to safety standards, including the adoption of new technologies, the strengthening of emergency preparedness, and the improvement of risk assessment and management practices.

The Fukushima disaster also raised important questions about the role of nuclear energy in the context of global efforts to address climate change. While nuclear power remains a significant source of low-carbon energy, the disaster underscored the need to carefully weigh the risks and benefits of nuclear energy and to explore alternative energy sources that can provide reliable and sustainable power without the associated risks.

In Japan, the disaster has had a lasting impact on public opinion and energy policy. The government has struggled to balance the need for energy security with the demands of a population that remains deeply skeptical of nuclear power. While some reactors have been restarted after undergoing safety upgrades, the future of nuclear energy in Japan remains uncertain, with ongoing debates about the role of renewables, the need for energy efficiency, and the pursuit of new energy technologies.

Chapter 3: Chernobyl Disaster

The Chernobyl disaster, which occurred on April 26, 1986, in the then-Soviet Union, remains the most catastrophic nuclear accident in history. The event took place at the Chernobyl Nuclear Power Plant near the town of Pripyat, in what is now Ukraine. This disaster not only caused significant immediate damage and loss of life but also had long-lasting environmental, health, socio-economic, and political consequences that continue to affect the region and the world to this day.

The Chernobyl Nuclear Power Plant: Background and Design

The Chernobyl Nuclear Power Plant was built in the 1970s and early 1980s as part of the Soviet Union's ambitious nuclear energy program. The plant used RBMK (Reaktor Bolshoy Moshchnosti Kanalny) reactors, a type of nuclear reactor designed in the Soviet Union. The RBMK reactor was a unique design that used graphite as a neutron moderator and water as a coolant. The reactors were chosen for their ability to produce both electricity and weapons-grade plutonium, which was in line with Soviet military and industrial goals.

However, the RBMK design had several critical flaws that contributed to the disaster. One of the most significant issues was the reactor's positive void coefficient, which meant that as the water turned to steam (voids), the nuclear reaction became more intense. This characteristic made the reactor unstable at low power levels. Additionally, the RBMK reactors lacked a robust containment structure, a feature common in Western reactor designs, which could have mitigated the release of radiation in the event of an accident.

The Lead-Up to the Disaster: A Test Goes Wrong

The Chernobyl disaster occurred during a safety test designed to simulate a power outage at Reactor 4. The test aimed to determine whether the reactor's turbines could provide enough electrical power to keep the cooling water pumps running during the brief period between the loss of external power and the start-up of emergency generators. The test had been conducted on the reactor before, but the previous tests had been unsuccessful.

The test was scheduled to take place during the day shift on April 25, 1986, but a delay in the shutdown of the reactor extended the test into the night shift. The night shift was less experienced, and the operators were not fully aware of the test's implications or the potential dangers involved.

The operators made a series of critical errors in preparing for the test. They disabled several safety systems, including the automatic shutdown mechanisms, to prevent the test from being interrupted. They also reduced the reactor's power level too quickly, causing it to become unstable. When the power level dropped too low, the operators attempted to restore it, but the reactor became increasingly unstable.

The Explosion: A Catastrophic Failure

At 1:23 AM on April 26, 1986, the test began, but within seconds, things went catastrophically wrong. A sudden power surge occurred in Reactor 4, leading to a massive increase in the reactor's temperature. The intense heat caused the reactor's fuel rods to rupture, and the steam pressure built up to the point where it blew the 1,000-ton reactor lid off, destroying the reactor building.

The explosion sent a massive cloud of radioactive material into the atmosphere, including isotopes such as iodine-131, cesium-137, and strontium-90. The force of the explosion also ignited a fire that burned for 10 days, releasing even more radioactive material into the environment.

Immediate Response: Chaos and Confusion

In the immediate aftermath of the explosion, there was confusion and denial about the severity of the situation. The plant workers and first responders were not fully informed about the dangers of radiation exposure, and many of them worked without adequate protective gear. Firefighters who arrived on the scene to extinguish the blaze were exposed to lethal doses of radiation. Many of these first responders, known as "liquidators," succumbed to acute radiation sickness within weeks of the disaster.

The Soviet authorities initially attempted to downplay the severity of the disaster. It wasn't until two days later, on April 28, 1986, when radiation detectors at a nuclear power plant in Sweden detected unusually high levels of radiation, that the international community became aware of the incident. The Soviet government was forced to acknowledge the accident, and evacuations began in the surrounding areas.

Evacuation and Exclusion Zone: A Ghost Town Emerges

The town of Pripyat, home to nearly 50,000 people, was evacuated on the afternoon of April 27, 1986, a full day after the explosion. Residents were told that the evacuation would be temporary, lasting only a few days. They left behind their homes, belongings, and lives, not knowing that they would never return.

The area around the Chernobyl plant, known as the Exclusion Zone, was expanded over the following weeks and months as the extent of the radioactive contamination became clearer. Eventually, an area with a radius of 30 kilometers (about 19 miles) around the plant was declared uninhabitable. The Exclusion Zone remains largely deserted to this day, with only a few thousand people, mostly elderly residents who refused to leave, still living within its boundaries.

The Human Toll: Health Impacts and Radiation Exposure

The immediate health effects of the Chernobyl disaster were severe for those directly exposed to high levels of radiation. Of the plant workers and first responders, 134 were diagnosed with acute radiation sickness, and 28 of them died within weeks of the disaster. The long-term health effects are still being studied and debated, but there is no doubt that the disaster had a profound impact on the health of millions of people.

One of the most significant health impacts was the dramatic increase in thyroid cancer, particularly among children and adolescents who were exposed to radioactive iodine-131. The World Health Organization (WHO) estimates that there have been thousands of cases of thyroid cancer linked to the disaster, many of which could have been prevented if iodine tablets had been distributed immediately following the explosion.

In addition to thyroid cancer, there has been an increase in other cancers, cardiovascular diseases, and mental health issues among those exposed to radiation. The psychological impact of the disaster, including stress, anxiety, and depression, has been significant, particularly among those who were evacuated and displaced from their homes.

Environmental Impact: A Contaminated Landscape

The environmental impact of the Chernobyl disaster was widespread and devastating. The radioactive fallout contaminated large areas of Ukraine, Belarus, and Russia, as well as parts of Europe. The most affected areas became known as "hot spots," where the levels of radiation were particularly high.

Forests, rivers, lakes, and farmland were all contaminated with radioactive isotopes. The so-called "Red Forest," located near the plant, is one of the most heavily contaminated areas. The explosion killed the trees almost instantly, turning the forest a reddish-brown color. Although the forest has since regrown, it remains highly radioactive.

The contamination of the soil and water had a profound impact on agriculture and food production in the affected areas. Crops, livestock, and fish were all contaminated with radioactive materials, leading to restrictions on the consumption of locally produced food. These restrictions have had long-term economic and social consequences for the communities living near the Exclusion Zone.

The radioactive fallout also had a significant impact on wildlife in the region. Initially, many animals died from radiation exposure, but over time, the absence of human activity in the Exclusion Zone has allowed wildlife to flourish. The area has become a de facto wildlife sanctuary, with populations of wolves, bears, lynx, and other species thriving in the absence of human interference. However, many of these animals still carry high levels of radiation in their bodies, and the long-term effects on their health are still being studied.

The Soviet Response: Cover-Up and Clean-Up

In the immediate aftermath of the disaster, the Soviet government took a number of actions to contain the situation and mitigate the spread of radiation. One of the first measures was the construction of a concrete sarcophagus, known as the "Chernobyl Shelter," to encase Reactor 4 and contain the release of radioactive material. The sarcophagus was completed in November 1986, just six months after the disaster. While it provided some protection, it was only a temporary solution, and it began to deteriorate over time.

The Soviet government also launched a massive clean-up operation, involving hundreds of thousands of people, known as liquidators. These workers were tasked with decontaminating the affected areas, constructing the sarcophagus, and burying radioactive waste. The liquidators played a crucial role in mitigating the impact of the disaster, but many of them were exposed to high levels of radiation, and thousands have since suffered from health problems as a result.

The Soviet government initially attempted to cover up the full extent of the disaster, downplaying the severity of the radiation release and the potential health risks. It was not until the fall of the Soviet Union in 1991 that the full scale of the disaster became known to the world. The lack of transparency and the mishandling of the crisis contributed to a loss of trust in the Soviet government, both domestically and internationally.

International Response and Support

The Chernobyl disaster had a significant impact on the international community, leading to a reevaluation of nuclear safety standards and an increase in international cooperation on nuclear safety issues. The International Atomic Energy Agency (IAEA) played a key role in coordinating the international response and providing technical assistance to the Soviet Union.

In the years following the disaster, the international community provided financial and technical support for the construction of a new, more durable structure to replace the aging sarcophagus. The New Safe Confinement (NSC) structure, completed in 2016, is a massive steel arch designed to encase Reactor 4 and prevent the release of radioactive material for at least the next 100 years. The NSC was funded by the Chernobyl Shelter Fund, which was established by the European Bank for Reconstruction and Development (EBRD) and supported by over 40 countries.

Long-Term Consequences: Health, Environment, and Politics

The long-term consequences of the Chernobyl disaster are still being felt today, more than three decades after the event. The health effects of radiation exposure continue to be studied, with ongoing debates about the true extent of the impact. Some estimates suggest that the disaster could eventually be responsible for tens of thousands of premature deaths, primarily due to cancer and other radiation-related diseases.

The environmental impact of the disaster is also ongoing. The Exclusion Zone remains highly contaminated, and it is likely to remain uninhabitable for centuries. However, the zone has also become an important site for scientific research, with studies focusing on the effects of radiation on ecosystems and the long-term impact of nuclear accidents on the environment.

The disaster also had significant political consequences, both in the Soviet Union and around the world. In the Soviet Union, the mishandling of the disaster contributed to growing public discontent with the government and played a role in the eventual collapse of the Soviet Union in 1991. Internationally, the disaster led to increased scrutiny of nuclear energy and a push for stronger safety regulations. Many countries reevaluated their nuclear energy programs in the wake of Chernobyl, and some, like Germany, decided to phase out nuclear power altogether.

Legacy of Chernobyl: A Cautionary Tale

The Chernobyl disaster serves as a powerful reminder of the dangers of nuclear energy and the catastrophic consequences of human error and technological failure. It highlighted the importance of rigorous safety standards, transparency, and international cooperation in the field of nuclear energy.

The disaster also underscored the need for better preparedness and response mechanisms in the event of a nuclear accident. The lessons learned from Chernobyl have been used to improve nuclear safety and emergency response protocols around the world. However, the risks associated with nuclear energy remain, as evidenced by the Fukushima Daiichi nuclear disaster in Japan in 2011, which was triggered by a massive earthquake and tsunami.

Despite the progress made in nuclear safety since Chernobyl, the disaster continues to cast a long shadow over the nuclear industry. It has become a symbol of the potential dangers of nuclear power and a cautionary tale about the consequences of complacency and the failure to adequately address safety concerns.

Chapter 4: Windscale Fire

The Windscale Fire, which occurred on October 10, 1957, remains one of the most significant nuclear accidents in British history. The event took place at the Windscale facility, now known as Sellafield, in Cumbria, England. This disaster not only had profound immediate effects on public health and the environment but also contributed to changes in the nuclear industry and regulations in the United Kingdom and beyond.

Windscale: Background and Context

Windscale was part of Britain's post-war nuclear program, which was initiated in the late 1940s. The primary purpose of the Windscale facility was to produce plutonium for the country's burgeoning nuclear weapons program. The facility housed two reactors, known as Windscale Pile 1 and Windscale Pile 2, which were air-cooled, graphite-moderated reactors designed to convert natural uranium into weapons-grade plutonium.

The Windscale reactors were some of the first of their kind in the world, and they were built under significant pressure. The United Kingdom was eager to develop its own nuclear arsenal to maintain its status as a global power, and the Windscale reactors were a crucial part of this strategy. However, the haste with which the reactors were constructed, coupled with limited understanding of the potential hazards, led to several design flaws that would later contribute to the disaster.

The reactors were encased in concrete, and they relied on a system of air cooling rather than the more modern water or gas cooling methods used in later reactors. The air was drawn in from the atmosphere, passed through the reactor to cool the graphite core and the fuel elements, and then released back into the environment through tall chimneys equipped with filters to capture radioactive particles. The reactors operated at relatively low temperatures compared to modern reactors, but the combination of air cooling and the use of graphite as a moderator introduced specific risks.

The Buildup to the Disaster: Wigner Energy and Reactor Behavior

One of the critical issues with the Windscale reactors was related to a phenomenon known as Wigner energy. Wigner energy, named after physicist Eugene Wigner, is the energy stored in the graphite moderator of a nuclear reactor due to the displacement of carbon atoms by neutron radiation. Over time, this stored energy can accumulate and, if not properly managed, can lead to an uncontrolled release of energy in the form of heat.

In the Windscale reactors, the buildup of Wigner energy was a known issue. To prevent the graphite from reaching dangerously high temperatures, the reactors periodically underwent a process called "annealing." Annealing involved raising the temperature of the reactor in a controlled manner to release the stored Wigner energy gradually. However, the process was not without risks, as it required precise control over the reactor's temperature and power levels.

By 1957, Windscale Pile 1 had undergone several annealing cycles, but there were growing concerns among the reactor operators about the increasing frequency with which these cycles were needed. The annealing process was not fully understood, and there were disagreements among the operators and engineers about the best way to manage the Wigner energy buildup. This lack of consensus, combined with the experimental nature of the reactors, set the stage for the disaster.

The Incident: How the Fire Started

The disaster began during an annealing process on October 7, 1957. The operators of Windscale Pile 1 initiated the annealing cycle as usual, intending to gradually raise the temperature of the reactor to release the Wigner energy. However, this particular annealing cycle did not proceed as expected.

During the annealing process, the reactor's temperature increased more rapidly than anticipated. The operators attempted to reduce the temperature by adjusting the control rods and lowering the reactor's power level, but these efforts were unsuccessful. Unknown to the operators, a localized hot spot had developed within the reactor's graphite core.

As the temperature continued to rise, the heat ignited the uranium fuel cartridges within the reactor. The design of the reactor contributed to the severity of the fire; the air-cooling system provided a continuous supply of oxygen, which fueled the flames. The fire quickly spread through the graphite core, reaching temperatures of up to 1,300 degrees Celsius (2,372 degrees Fahrenheit).

The operators initially did not realize that a fire had started inside the reactor. The lack of direct visual monitoring inside the reactor core and the limitations of the available instrumentation made it difficult to assess the situation. It was only when radiation levels in the facility began to rise alarmingly, and an increase in temperature readings was observed, that the operators recognized the gravity of the situation.

The Struggle to Contain the Fire: Emergency Response Efforts

Once it was clear that a fire had broken out in the reactor, the operators and emergency response teams faced an unprecedented and highly dangerous situation. The primary concern was the potential release of radioactive material into the atmosphere, which could have devastating consequences for public health and the environment.

The first step in the emergency response was to shut down the reactor by fully inserting the control rods, which were designed to absorb neutrons and stop the nuclear reaction. However, this action did not immediately extinguish the fire, as the heat continued to rise due to the ongoing combustion of the graphite and uranium.

The reactor's cooling system was still operational, and the operators increased the flow of air through the reactor in an attempt to cool the core. However, this only made the situation worse by providing additional oxygen to the fire, which continued to burn intensely.

As the situation deteriorated, the operators considered flooding the reactor with water to extinguish the fire. This was a highly risky maneuver because the interaction of water with the hot graphite and uranium could potentially lead to a steam explosion, further spreading radioactive material. Despite the risks, the operators began to introduce water into the reactor core on October 10.

Fortunately, the introduction of water, combined with a reduction in the air supply, eventually helped to bring the fire under control. By the evening of October 10, the flames had subsided, and the temperature in the reactor began to decrease. However, the damage had already been done, and the fire had caused a significant release of radioactive material into the atmosphere.

The Release of Radioactive Material: Environmental and Health Impacts

The Windscale fire released a substantial amount of radioactive material, including iodine-131, cesium-137, and xenon-133, into the atmosphere. The radioactive cloud spread across the United Kingdom and even reached parts of mainland Europe. The most significant release was of iodine-131, a radioactive isotope that accumulates in the thyroid gland and can cause thyroid cancer.

In the immediate aftermath of the fire, the British government and the operators of Windscale took steps to minimize the impact of the radioactive release. The milk from cows grazing in the areas downwind of the reactor was found to be contaminated with iodine-131, and as a precautionary measure, the government ordered the destruction of milk produced within a 200-square-mile (520-square-kilometer) area around the site. Approximately two million liters of milk were discarded to reduce the public's exposure to radiation.

Despite these efforts, it is estimated that several hundred people may have developed thyroid cancer as a result of exposure to the iodine-131 released during the fire. The full extent of the health impacts remains uncertain, as the long-term consequences of the radiation exposure are difficult to quantify.

The environmental impact of the Windscale fire was also significant. The surrounding countryside was contaminated with radioactive isotopes, and the cleanup of the site took several years. Although the immediate area around the Windscale facility was heavily contaminated, the wider environmental impact was somewhat mitigated by the prevailing winds, which dispersed the radioactive cloud over a large area.

The Investigation and Aftermath: Lessons Learned

In the aftermath of the Windscale fire, a comprehensive investigation was launched to determine the causes of the disaster and to prevent similar incidents in the future. The inquiry revealed several critical flaws in the design and operation of the Windscale reactors.

One of the primary issues identified was the lack of understanding of Wigner energy and its potential to cause dangerous temperature increases within the reactor core. The investigation also highlighted the inadequacies of the reactor's cooling system and the lack of effective safety measures to deal with a fire of this magnitude.

The inquiry resulted in several important recommendations for improving nuclear safety. Among these was the need for better monitoring and control systems to detect and respond to dangerous conditions within the reactor core. The inquiry also recommended changes to the design and operation of nuclear reactors to reduce the risk of similar incidents in the future.

The Windscale fire also had significant political and public relations consequences. The British government was criticized for its handling of the disaster and for the lack of transparency in communicating the risks to the public. The incident led to increased public skepticism about nuclear energy and contributed to a more cautious approach to nuclear power development in the United Kingdom.

Long-Term Impact and Legacy

The Windscale fire had a lasting impact on the nuclear industry in the United Kingdom and around the world. It served as a stark reminder of the potential dangers of nuclear energy and the need for stringent safety measures and oversight.

One of the most significant long-term impacts of the Windscale fire was the changes it prompted in nuclear safety regulations. The disaster led to the establishment of more rigorous safety standards for the design, operation, and maintenance of nuclear reactors. It also contributed to the development of more robust emergency response protocols and the creation of independent regulatory bodies to oversee nuclear safety.

The Windscale fire also influenced public opinion about nuclear energy. In the years following the disaster, there was a growing public awareness of the risks associated with nuclear power, and this awareness contributed to the rise of the anti-nuclear movement in the United Kingdom and other countries. The incident also had an impact on the nuclear policies of other nations, with some countries re-evaluating their nuclear programs in light of the lessons learned from Windscale.

Despite the negative consequences of the disaster, the Windscale fire also contributed to important advances in nuclear science and engineering. The lessons learned from the incident helped to improve the understanding of reactor behavior, particularly the management of Wigner energy and the risks associated with graphite-moderated reactors. These advances have contributed to the development of safer and more reliable nuclear technologies.

Chapter 5: Tokaimura Nuclear Accident

The Tokaimura nuclear accident, which occurred on September 30, 1999, is one of Japan's most serious nuclear incidents. Taking place in Tokai, Ibaraki Prefecture, this accident is notable for being a criticality event—a rare and dangerous type of nuclear accident where a chain reaction becomes self-sustaining, leading to the uncontrolled release of radiation. The incident exposed severe flaws in safety protocols, operational oversight, and crisis management within Japan's nuclear industry, leaving an indelible mark on the country's approach to nuclear safety.

Background of the Tokaimura Facility: A Site with a History of Nuclear Activity

Tokaimura, often referred to simply as Tokai, is a small village in Ibaraki Prefecture, located about 140 kilometers northeast of Tokyo. Despite its modest size, Tokaimura has been a focal point of Japan's nuclear industry since the 1950s. The village became home to Japan's first commercial nuclear reactor, and over the decades, it developed into a hub for various nuclear-related activities, including research, power generation, and fuel processing.

The facility involved in the 1999 accident was operated by JCO (formerly Japan Nuclear Fuel Conversion Co.), a subsidiary of Sumitomo Metal Mining Co. This plant was primarily involved in the production of uranium fuel for nuclear reactors. It specialized in converting uranium hexafluoride (UF6) into uranium dioxide (UO2) and uranium nitrate, materials used in the production of nuclear fuel.

The particular process that led to the accident was the conversion of enriched uranium into uranium dioxide for use in a fast breeder reactor. The uranium being handled during the incident was enriched to a concentration of around 18.8% uranium-235, significantly higher than the typical enrichment level of around 3-5% used in most commercial nuclear reactors. This higher enrichment level made the material more susceptible to reaching criticality if not handled under strict controls.

The Sequence of Events: A Series of Errors Leading to Criticality

The accident at Tokaimura was the result of a series of procedural violations and human errors that culminated in a criticality incident. The root cause of the disaster can be traced to the breakdown of safety protocols, improper training of workers, and a culture that prioritized speed and efficiency over adherence to safety regulations.

On the morning of September 30, 1999, three workers at the JCO plant were tasked with preparing a batch of uranium fuel for use in the fast breeder reactor. This involved dissolving uranium oxide powder in nitric acid to produce uranium nitrate. The process required the uranium nitrate solution to be carefully controlled to prevent it from reaching critical mass—a condition where the nuclear chain reaction becomes self-sustaining.

The standard procedure called for the uranium nitrate solution to be mixed in a specially designed dissolution tank that was engineered to prevent criticality by limiting the volume and shape of the solution. However, due to a combination of inadequate training and a desire to expedite the process, the workers deviated from the established protocol.

Instead of using the dissolution tank, the workers mixed the uranium nitrate solution in stainless steel buckets, a practice that was strictly prohibited due to the risk of criticality. As they poured the solution into a precipitation tank that was not designed to safely handle such high concentrations of uranium, they inadvertently created a configuration that allowed the solution to reach critical mass.

At approximately 10:35 AM, the solution reached criticality. A blue flash, characteristic of a criticality event, was observed by the workers, signaling that a self-sustaining nuclear chain reaction had begun. This reaction caused a burst of radiation to be emitted, exposing the workers to lethal doses of gamma rays and neutrons.

Immediate Consequences: Radiation Exposure and Emergency Response

The three workers—Hisashi Ouchi, Masato Shinohara, and Yutaka Yokokawa—were the first to experience the devastating effects of the radiation burst. Ouchi, who was closest to the tank, received the highest dose, estimated at around 17 sieverts (Sv), far beyond the lethal dose threshold. Shinohara and Yokokawa received doses of approximately 10 Sv and 3 Sv, respectively. For context, a dose of about 1 Sv can cause acute radiation sickness, and doses above 5 Sv are typically fatal without prompt medical intervention.

In the immediate aftermath of the criticality event, the workers reported feeling intense pain, nausea, and difficulty breathing. Realizing the severity of the situation, they quickly evacuated the area and alerted their supervisors. However, the chain reaction within the tank continued intermittently for nearly 20 hours, releasing more radiation into the environment.

The plant's emergency response was delayed and poorly coordinated. There was confusion among the staff about the nature of the incident, and it took some time for the magnitude of the radiation release to be fully understood. The local authorities were notified, and an evacuation was ordered for residents within a 350-meter radius of the plant. The affected area was later expanded to a 10-kilometer radius, affecting around 310,000 people.

Emergency response teams, including the Japan Atomic Energy Research Institute (JAERI), the Self-Defense Forces, and local fire departments, were mobilized to contain the incident. They worked to stop the nuclear reaction by draining the cooling water from the precipitation tank, which helped to absorb the neutrons and bring the reaction under control. By the morning of October 1, the reaction had finally ceased.

Medical Treatment of the Victims: A Struggle for Survival

The three workers were immediately transported to the National Institute of Radiological Sciences in Chiba for treatment. Given the unprecedented levels of radiation exposure, their cases presented significant challenges to the medical team.

Hisashi Ouchi, who had received the highest dose, was in critical condition. His body suffered from severe radiation burns, and his internal organs were failing. Radiation had destroyed his bone marrow, leaving him unable to produce new blood cells. Despite aggressive treatments, including skin grafts, blood transfusions, and experimental stem cell therapy, Ouchi's condition continued to deteriorate.

Ouchi endured 83 days of excruciating pain before he succumbed to multiple organ failure on December 21, 1999. His prolonged suffering raised ethical questions about the extent to which life-prolonging measures should be pursued in cases of severe radiation exposure.

Masato Shinohara, who received a slightly lower dose of radiation, also suffered from acute radiation sickness. He underwent multiple treatments, including bone marrow transplants, but ultimately died of multiple organ failure on April 27, 2000, after nearly seven months of battling the effects of the radiation.

Yutaka Yokokawa, who was exposed to the lowest dose among the three, survived but suffered from long-term health effects, including chronic pain, fatigue, and psychological trauma. He spent several months in the hospital and underwent extensive rehabilitation.

The Environmental Impact: Contamination and Cleanup Efforts

The Tokaimura accident had significant environmental repercussions, particularly concerning radioactive contamination. The criticality event released a substantial amount of radiation into the air, including fission products such as iodine-131, cesium-137, and xenon-133. These radioactive isotopes dispersed into the surrounding area, contaminating the atmosphere, soil, and water sources.

One of the most immediate concerns was the potential contamination of food and water supplies. The Japanese government conducted extensive monitoring of radiation levels in the air, soil, and water within the evacuation zone and beyond. While the levels of contamination were relatively low compared to other nuclear accidents like Chernobyl or Fukushima, they were nonetheless significant enough to warrant precautionary measures.

The contaminated area around the JCO plant was cordoned off, and efforts were made to decontaminate the site. This involved removing and safely disposing of contaminated soil, cleaning up affected buildings and equipment, and monitoring radiation levels to ensure they were within acceptable limits. The cleanup process took several months, during which time access to the plant was strictly controlled.

The long-term environmental impact of the Tokaimura accident is less severe than that of larger-scale nuclear disasters, but the incident still left a legacy of contamination and concern among the local population. The psychological impact on the residents, many of whom were forced to evacuate their homes, was profound, and the incident contributed to a growing sense of mistrust in the nuclear industry.

The Investigation and Legal Proceedings: Uncovering the Failures

In the aftermath of the Tokaimura accident, a thorough investigation was launched to determine the causes of the disaster and to assign responsibility. The investigation revealed a series of critical failures at multiple levels, from operational procedures to regulatory oversight.

One of the most glaring issues identified was the deviation from standard operating procedures by the workers. The use of stainless-steel buckets to mix uranium nitrate solution was a clear violation of safety protocols, yet it was a practice that had become routine at the plant. This breach of protocol was not an isolated incident but rather a symptom of a broader culture of complacency and corner-cutting within the company.

The investigation also highlighted the lack of proper training and education for the workers involved in handling nuclear materials. Many of the workers, including those involved in the criticality incident, were not fully aware of the risks associated with their tasks or the reasons behind the established safety protocols. This lack of knowledge contributed to their willingness to bypass procedures that were designed to prevent exactly the kind of accident that occurred.

Furthermore, the investigation pointed to serious deficiencies in the regulatory oversight of the Tokaimura facility. The Japanese regulatory authorities, including the Science and Technology Agency (STA) and the Nuclear Safety Commission (NSC), were criticized for failing to adequately enforce safety standards and for allowing unsafe practices to persist at the JCO plant. The regulators were also faulted for not conducting sufficient inspections and for being overly reliant on self-reporting by the company.

In the legal proceedings that followed, six JCO officials, including plant managers and company executives, were charged with professional negligence resulting in death. The court found that the company had failed to implement proper safety measures and that the negligence of its employees directly contributed to the accident. In 2003, the court handed down sentences ranging from suspended prison terms to fines, but the penalties were criticized by some as being too lenient given the severity of the incident.

The Aftermath and Lessons Learned: A Turning Point for Japan's Nuclear Industry

The Tokaimura nuclear accident had profound implications for Japan's nuclear industry and its regulatory framework. In the immediate aftermath, there was a significant loss of public trust in the nuclear sector, and the incident sparked widespread fear and anxiety about the safety of nuclear facilities in Japan.

The government responded by overhauling its regulatory approach to nuclear safety. This included the establishment of stricter safety standards, increased oversight, and more rigorous inspections of nuclear facilities. The Science and Technology Agency was reorganized, and the Nuclear Safety Commission was given greater authority to enforce regulations and ensure compliance.

The Tokaimura incident also led to a reassessment of the safety culture within the nuclear industry. There was a renewed emphasis on the importance of training and education for nuclear workers, particularly in understanding the criticality risks associated with the handling of fissile materials. Companies were required to implement more robust safety protocols and to foster a culture of safety that prioritized adherence to procedures over efficiency or cost-cutting.

Internationally, the Tokaimura accident served as a cautionary tale about the dangers of criticality events and the need for rigorous safety measures when handling enriched uranium. The incident was studied by nuclear safety experts around the world, and it contributed to the development of better training programs, improved safety standards, and enhanced crisis management protocols.

Chapter 6: Kyshtym Disaster

The Kyshtym disaster, which occurred on September 29, 1957, in the Soviet Union, is one of the most significant and least known nuclear accidents in history. Named after the nearby town of Kyshtym in the Chelyabinsk region, the disaster took place at the Mayak Production Association, a secretive nuclear facility that was a key part of the Soviet Union's nuclear weapons program. Although it is less famous than the Chernobyl or Fukushima disasters, the Kyshtym disaster ranks as one of the most severe nuclear accidents, with widespread environmental contamination and long-lasting health effects for the affected population. The event was shrouded in secrecy for decades due to the Cold War context, making it one of the most hidden nuclear tragedies in history.

The Mayak Production Association: A History of Secrecy and Nuclear Ambitions

The Mayak facility, located near the town of Ozyorsk (then known as Chelyabinsk-40), was established in the late 1940s as part of the Soviet Union's efforts to develop nuclear weapons. The facility was one of the USSR's primary centers for plutonium production, crucial for the creation of nuclear bombs. Built rapidly in the aftermath of World War II, Mayak was a top-secret installation, hidden from public knowledge and even from most government officials.

The conditions under which Mayak was constructed and operated were perilous. In the rush to produce nuclear weapons, safety considerations were often neglected. Workers at Mayak were exposed to high levels of radiation without adequate protection, and the facility's waste management practices were dangerously inadequate. Liquid radioactive waste was routinely discharged into nearby rivers, contaminating water sources and ecosystems. Solid radioactive waste was stored in makeshift facilities, often without proper containment.

By the mid-1950s, Mayak had produced significant quantities of plutonium, but the accumulation of radioactive waste at the site had become a severe problem. The waste was stored in large tanks, some of which were cooled by water to prevent overheating. However, the infrastructure for waste management was rudimentary and poorly maintained, setting the stage for a catastrophic failure.

The Sequence of Events Leading to the Disaster

The disaster at Kyshtym was the result of a failure in the cooling system of one of the waste storage tanks at the Mayak facility. This particular tank, which contained about 70-80 tons of highly radioactive liquid waste, was equipped with a cooling system designed to prevent the waste from overheating. However, in the summer of 1956, the cooling system malfunctioned, and the temperature inside the tank began to rise.

Despite the increasing temperature and the growing risk of an explosion, the problem went unnoticed for several months. The Soviet Union's emphasis on secrecy and the compartmentalization of information within the nuclear program meant that critical safety concerns were often ignored or downplayed. Workers at Mayak were not informed about the potential dangers, and no measures were taken to address the cooling system failure.

By September 1957, the temperature inside the tank had reached critical levels. On September 29, 1957, at around 4:20 PM local time, the tank exploded with a force equivalent to about 70-100 tons of TNT. The explosion was non-nuclear but was caused by the chemical reaction of the overheated waste. The blast destroyed the storage facility and released a massive cloud of radioactive material into the atmosphere.

The explosion released approximately 20 million curies (740 PBq) of radioactivity, making it one of the largest releases of radioactive material in history. The radioactive cloud, containing a mixture of fission products, including strontium-90, cesium-137, and other isotopes, was carried by the wind over a large area, creating a radioactive plume that spread contamination over hundreds of kilometers.

The Environmental Impact: Contamination and the Creation of the East-Ural Radioactive Trace (EURT)

The explosion at Mayak and the subsequent release of radioactive material created a contamination zone that became known as the East-Ural Radioactive Trace (EURT). The EURT extended northeast from the Mayak facility, covering an area of about 20,000 square kilometers. The contamination primarily affected the Chelyabinsk, Sverdlovsk, and Tyumen regions, with the most heavily contaminated area being a strip about 300 kilometers long and 50 kilometers wide.

The radioactive fallout from the Kyshtym disaster contaminated the soil, water, and vegetation in the affected areas. Strontium-90 and cesium-137, two of the most dangerous isotopes released, have long half-lives and pose significant health risks due to their ability to be absorbed by living organisms. Strontium-90, for example, is chemically similar to calcium and can be incorporated into bones, where it emits radiation and increases the risk of bone cancer and leukemia.

The contamination of agricultural land was particularly devastating. Crops and livestock in the affected regions absorbed radioactive isotopes, leading to the internal contamination of the local population through the consumption of contaminated food and water. The extent of the environmental damage was so severe that the Soviet authorities eventually had to evacuate several villages and declare large areas as uninhabitable.

The Mayak facility itself was heavily contaminated by the explosion, and the surrounding area became one of the most polluted places on Earth. The contamination of the Techa River, into which radioactive waste had been discharged for years before the disaster, was exacerbated by the Kyshtym explosion, leading to further environmental degradation and health problems for communities living downstream.

The Human Impact: Health Consequences and the Plight of the Affected Population

The Kyshtym disaster had severe and long-lasting health consequences for the people living in the affected regions. The immediate impact of the radioactive release was felt by the workers at Mayak and the residents of nearby villages, many of whom were exposed to high levels of radiation without any warning or protection.

In the days following the explosion, people living in the contamination zone began to experience symptoms of acute radiation sickness (ARS), including nausea, vomiting, hair loss, and severe burns. The Soviet authorities, however, were slow to respond to the crisis. The secrecy surrounding the Mayak facility and the government's desire to avoid public panic led to a delayed and inadequate evacuation of the affected population.

It is estimated that around 10,000 people were evacuated from the most heavily contaminated areas, but many more remained in the affected zone without proper information or protection. The evacuation itself was poorly managed, with some residents being moved to areas that were still contaminated. The lack of medical facilities and trained personnel in the region further exacerbated the situation, as those affected by radiation exposure struggled to receive adequate care.

In the years and decades following the disaster, the long-term health effects of radiation exposure became increasingly apparent. Rates of cancer, particularly thyroid cancer, leukemia, and bone cancer, increased significantly among the exposed population. Genetic mutations and birth defects also became more common in the affected areas, leading to a tragic legacy of suffering for future generations.

The Soviet government, keen to maintain the secrecy of its nuclear program, downplayed the disaster and its consequences. The full extent of the health impacts was not acknowledged until many years later, and the affected population received little compensation or support. It was only after the collapse of the Soviet Union that more information about the Kyshtym disaster and its human toll began to emerge.

The Soviet Response: Secrecy, Denial, and Limited Remediation Efforts

The Kyshtym disaster occurred during a period of intense secrecy in the Soviet Union, particularly regarding its nuclear program. The authorities' initial response to the disaster was characterized by a combination of denial, obfuscation, and minimal public disclosure. The Soviet government did not officially acknowledge the disaster until 1989, more than three decades after it occurred.

In the immediate aftermath of the explosion, the Soviet authorities imposed a strict information blackout. The local population was kept in the dark about the true nature of the disaster, and even within the Soviet leadership, details were closely guarded. The government feared that acknowledging the disaster would undermine public confidence in the Soviet nuclear program and provide ammunition for Western critics during the Cold War.

Despite the lack of public acknowledgment, the Soviet authorities did take some steps to address the contamination. The most heavily contaminated villages were evacuated, and the residents were resettled in other areas, though often without adequate compensation or support. The evacuated areas were cordoned off and designated as part of a restricted zone, known as the East-Ural Nature Reserve, which was intended to limit human access and prevent further exposure to radiation.

Within the Mayak facility itself, cleanup efforts were undertaken to decontaminate the site and prevent further releases of radioactive material. However, these efforts were limited by the lack of proper technology and resources, and the area around Mayak remained highly contaminated. The long-term environmental remediation of the affected region was not seriously pursued until after the collapse of the Soviet Union, and even today, parts of the area remain contaminated.

The secrecy surrounding the disaster meant that the true scale of the contamination and its impact on human health was not widely known, even within the Soviet Union. The local population was largely left to fend for itself, with many people continuing to live in contaminated areas and suffer the consequences of radiation exposure. The lack of transparency and accountability from the Soviet government contributed to the enduring legacy of suffering caused by the Kyshtym disaster.

International Awareness and Recognition: A Hidden Tragedy Comes to Light

For many years, the Kyshtym disaster was virtually unknown outside the Soviet Union. The first hints of the disaster emerged in the early 1960s when reports of a mysterious radioactive cloud over the Ural Mountains began to circulate in the West. These reports were based on intelligence gathered by Western agencies and observations of increased radiation levels in the atmosphere, but the Soviet Union consistently denied that any major nuclear accident had occurred.

It was not until 1976 that the existence of the Kyshtym disaster was publicly confirmed by Zhores Medvedev, a Soviet biologist who defected to the West. Medvedev's book, "Nuclear Disaster in the Urals," provided detailed information about the disaster and the environmental and human toll it had taken. His revelations were initially met with skepticism, but over time, more evidence emerged to support his account.

In the years following Medvedev's revelations, the Kyshtym disaster gradually gained recognition as one of the world's most significant nuclear accidents. However, it remained overshadowed by more recent and more publicized disasters such as Chernobyl and Fukushima. The Kyshtym disaster's relative obscurity is partly due to the Soviet government's successful efforts to keep it hidden and the limited access to information during the Cold War.

After the collapse of the Soviet Union in 1991, more information about the Kyshtym disaster and its consequences became available. Declassified documents, scientific studies, and testimonies from survivors helped to paint a fuller picture of the disaster's impact. Today, the Kyshtym disaster is recognized as a major event in the history of nuclear energy, with important lessons for the management of nuclear waste, the importance of safety protocols, and the need for transparency and accountability in the nuclear industry.

Lessons Learned and the Legacy of the Kyshtym Disaster

The Kyshtym disaster serves as a stark reminder of the dangers associated with nuclear energy, particularly when safety is compromised for the sake of secrecy or expediency. The disaster highlighted the critical importance of proper waste management in nuclear facilities, as well as the need for robust cooling systems to prevent the overheating of radioactive materials.

One of the key lessons from the Kyshtym disaster is the importance of transparency and open communication in managing nuclear risks. The Soviet government's decision to keep the disaster secret and to withhold information from both the public and the international community exacerbated the disaster's impact and delayed the implementation of effective remediation measures. The lack of transparency also hindered the ability of the affected population to protect themselves from radiation exposure and contributed to the long-term health consequences of the disaster.

The Kyshtym disaster also underscores the need for strong regulatory oversight of nuclear facilities. The conditions at the Mayak facility, where safety was often neglected in the rush to produce plutonium, were a recipe for disaster. Effective regulation and enforcement of safety standards are essential to prevent similar accidents in the future.

In the years since the Kyshtym disaster, the nuclear industry has made significant strides in improving safety and waste management practices. However, the legacy of Kyshtym serves as a cautionary tale about the potential consequences of complacency and the need for constant vigilance in the nuclear sector.

Chapter 7: Maxey Flats Nuclear Disposal Site Contamination

The Maxey Flats Nuclear Disposal Site, located in northeastern Kentucky, is one of the most infamous examples of nuclear waste mismanagement in the United States. The site, which was operational from 1963 to 1977, became a symbol of the environmental and public health risks associated with the disposal of radioactive materials. The story of Maxey Flats is a cautionary tale of regulatory oversight failures, environmental degradation, and the long-lasting consequences of improper nuclear waste disposal.

Background and Establishment of the Maxey Flats Site

In the early 1960s, as the United States expanded its nuclear power program, there was an increasing need for disposal sites for low-level radioactive waste. Low-level radioactive waste includes materials that have been contaminated with radioactive isotopes and are not classified as high-level waste, such as spent nuclear fuel. This waste is generated from a variety of sources, including nuclear power plants, medical facilities, research institutions, and industrial processes.

Maxey Flats, a 252-acre site in Fleming County, Kentucky, was selected as one of several commercial low-level radioactive waste disposal sites across the country. The site was chosen due to its remote location, low population density, and the perceived stability of the surrounding geology. The site began operations in 1963 under the management of Nuclear Engineering Company (NECO), which was responsible for the disposal of radioactive waste.

Operations at Maxey Flats

During its 14 years of operation, Maxey Flats received over 5 million cubic feet of low-level radioactive waste from across the United States. The waste was buried in shallow, unlined trenches that were dug into the soil and bedrock. The trenches, which were typically 20 to 25 feet deep, were backfilled with soil after they were filled with waste. The waste included contaminated equipment, clothing, building materials, and other debris.

The design and operational practices at Maxey Flats were typical of the time, but they were later revealed to be inadequate for containing radioactive materials. The disposal method relied heavily on the assumption that the surrounding geology would prevent the migration of radioactive contaminants into the environment. However, this assumption would prove to be disastrously incorrect.

Contamination and Environmental Impact

The problems at Maxey Flats began to surface almost immediately after the site started operations. The first signs of trouble were reports of radioactive materials leaching from the disposal trenches into the surrounding soil and groundwater. The unlined trenches allowed rainwater to percolate through the waste, which facilitated the migration of radionuclides into the environment.

One of the most significant environmental impacts was the contamination of local groundwater. The Maxey Flats site is located in a region characterized by karst geology, which includes underground limestone formations with extensive networks of fractures and sinkholes. This type of geology is highly permeable and prone to the rapid movement of water, making it particularly unsuitable for containing hazardous waste.

As a result, radioactive contaminants, including tritium, strontium-90, cesium-137, and plutonium, began to spread through the groundwater and surface water in the area. The contamination was not confined to the site itself but extended to nearby streams, rivers, and agricultural land, threatening the health of local residents and the environment.

Regulatory Oversight and Response

The regulatory oversight of Maxey Flats during its operational years was minimal and largely ineffective. The Atomic Energy Commission (AEC), which was responsible for overseeing the disposal of radioactive waste at the time, had limited resources and expertise to manage the growing number of disposal sites across the country. The AEC largely relied on the operators of these sites to self-regulate and report any issues, which created a significant conflict of interest.

Throughout the 1960s and 1970s, concerns about the safety and environmental impact of Maxey Flats grew. Local residents, environmental groups, and some government officials began to raise alarms about the contamination and the potential health risks associated with the site. However, it wasn't until the mid-1970s that the full extent of the problem became apparent.

In 1975, the AEC conducted a comprehensive investigation of the Maxey Flats site, which revealed widespread contamination and serious deficiencies in the site's design and operation. The investigation found that the trenches were leaking radioactive materials into the groundwater and that the site was not adequately secured to prevent unauthorized access. The AEC's findings prompted a series of actions aimed at mitigating the contamination and preventing further environmental damage.

Closure and Cleanup Efforts

Faced with mounting evidence of environmental contamination and public health risks, the Maxey Flats site was ordered to cease operations in 1977. The site was officially closed in 1978, but the closure marked the beginning of a decades-long cleanup and remediation effort that continues to this day.

The initial response to the contamination involved a series of containment measures aimed at preventing further migration of radioactive materials. These measures included capping the trenches with clay and other impermeable materials to reduce the infiltration of rainwater, installing a system of groundwater monitoring wells, and constructing barriers to control the flow of contaminated water.

Despite these efforts, the contamination at Maxey Flats proved to be more persistent and widespread than initially anticipated. The site continued to pose a significant environmental risk, and more comprehensive remediation efforts were required. In the 1980s and 1990s, the U.S. Environmental Protection Agency (EPA) and the U.S. Department of Energy (DOE) took over the management of the site and initiated a series of long-term cleanup projects.

The Superfund Designation and Remediation Efforts

In 1986, Maxey Flats was added to the National Priorities List (NPL), making it a Superfund site. The Superfund program, established under the Comprehensive Environmental Response, Compensation, and Liability Act (CERCLA) of 1980, was designed to address the most hazardous waste sites in the United States and to ensure that responsible parties are held accountable for cleanup costs.

The Superfund designation marked a turning point in the cleanup of Maxey Flats. The EPA and DOE developed a comprehensive remediation plan that included a range of measures to contain the contamination and protect public health and the environment. These measures included:

1. **Capping and Containment:** The site was capped with a

multi-layer cover system designed to prevent rainwater infiltration and reduce the spread of radioactive materials. The cover system included layers of clay, geotextile fabric, and topsoil, and it was designed to last for several hundred years.

2. **Groundwater Monitoring and Treatment:** A network of monitoring wells was installed to track the movement of contaminants in the groundwater. The groundwater was treated to remove radioactive materials before it was discharged into the environment. The monitoring and treatment system was designed to operate indefinitely.

3. **Institutional Controls:** To prevent future use or development of the contaminated land, the EPA implemented institutional controls, including land use restrictions and deed notices. These controls are intended to protect public health by ensuring that the site is not used for residential, agricultural, or recreational purposes.

4. **Long-Term Surveillance and Maintenance:** The EPA and DOE established a long-term surveillance and maintenance plan for Maxey Flats, which includes regular inspections, monitoring, and maintenance of the cap, groundwater treatment systems, and other containment measures. This plan is designed to ensure the long-term stability and safety of the site.

Health and Environmental Impacts

The health and environmental impacts of the Maxey Flats contamination have been the subject of extensive study and concern. The site's proximity to residential areas, agricultural land, and water sources raised serious questions about the potential exposure of local residents to radioactive materials.

Studies conducted in the years following the closure of Maxey Flats have documented elevated levels of radioactivity in the groundwater, surface water, and soil in the surrounding area. The contamination posed risks to both human health and the environment, including the potential for increased cancer rates, genetic mutations, and other health problems among exposed populations.

One of the most significant concerns was the potential for long-term exposure to low levels of radiation. While the immediate health effects of radiation exposure are well-documented, the long-term effects of chronic, low-level exposure are less well understood. This uncertainty has fueled ongoing debates about the adequacy of the cleanup efforts and the need for continued monitoring and protection.

The environmental impacts of the Maxey Flats contamination have also been profound. The spread of radioactive materials into local waterways and agricultural land has had long-lasting effects on the ecosystem. Contaminated water and soil can affect plant and animal life, potentially leading to bioaccumulation of radionuclides in the food chain and further spreading the contamination.

Ongoing Challenges and the Legacy of Maxey Flats

Despite the extensive cleanup efforts at Maxey Flats, challenges remain. The site continues to be a source of environmental concern, and the long-term stability of the containment measures is not guaranteed. The cap and other containment systems require ongoing maintenance and monitoring to ensure their effectiveness, and any failure of these systems could result in the release of radioactive materials into the environment.

Moreover, the Maxey Flats site serves as a stark reminder of the broader challenges associated with nuclear waste disposal. The site's history underscores the importance of selecting appropriate locations for waste disposal, designing robust containment systems, and maintaining rigorous regulatory oversight. The lessons learned from Maxey Flats have informed the development of more stringent regulations and best practices for nuclear waste disposal in the United States and around the world.

The legacy of Maxey Flats also highlights the ethical and social dimensions of nuclear waste management. The decision to locate a nuclear waste disposal site in a rural, economically disadvantaged area like Fleming County raises important questions about environmental justice and the fair distribution of environmental risks and benefits. The residents of Fleming County, many of whom were unaware of the risks associated with the site, have borne the brunt of the environmental and health impacts of the contamination.

Chapter 8: Goiania Accident

The Goiânia accident is one of the most severe incidents of radioactive contamination in history, occurring in September 1987 in the city of Goiânia, the capital of the state of Goiás in Brazil. This tragic event, often referred to as the "Goiânia disaster," resulted from the improper handling of a highly radioactive source that had been abandoned in an unsecured location. The incident led to the death of several people, significant contamination of the environment, and long-lasting social and psychological impacts on the affected community.

The Goiânia accident is a powerful reminder of the dangers associated with radioactive materials, particularly when they are not properly managed or secured. The event highlighted the critical importance of regulatory oversight, public awareness, and emergency preparedness in preventing and responding to radiological incidents. The story of Goiânia is also a poignant tale of human error, ignorance, and the tragic consequences that can arise when dangerous materials fall into the wrong hands.

Background: The Source of the Radiation

The Goiânia accident centers around a teletherapy unit, a piece of medical equipment used for radiation therapy to treat cancer. This particular teletherapy unit, which contained a highly radioactive isotope of cesium, specifically cesium-137, was originally housed in the Instituto Goiano de Radioterapia, a private radiotherapy institute located in Goiânia. The cesium-137 was encapsulated in a small cylinder within the teletherapy machine, which was designed to focus and direct the radiation for therapeutic purposes.

In 1985, the radiotherapy institute relocated to a new facility, leaving the old site, along with the teletherapy unit, abandoned and unattended. The owners of the institute were embroiled in a legal dispute over the property, and as a result, the teletherapy unit was never properly decommissioned or secured. It remained in the abandoned building for over two years, posing a significant but unnoticed risk to anyone who might come into contact with it.

Discovery of the Source: The Chain of Events

The disaster began on September 13, 1987, when two men, Roberto dos Santos Alves and Wagner Mota Pereira, both scavengers, entered the abandoned Instituto Goiano de Radioterapia in search of scrap metal that they could sell for money. Unaware of the dangers, they discovered the teletherapy unit and decided to take it with them, believing that the machine might contain valuable metal parts. They transported the unit to Roberto's home, where they began to dismantle it using simple tools.

As they worked to disassemble the machine, the men eventually reached the cylinder containing the cesium-137 source. They noticed that the cylinder emitted a faint blue glow in the dark, which they found intriguing but did not recognize as a sign of intense radioactivity. Over the next few days, the men continued to handle the cylinder, inadvertently contaminating themselves, their homes, and their surroundings with radioactive cesium.

Unaware of the danger, Roberto and Wagner began to share their discovery with friends, family, and neighbors. The glowing blue substance fascinated many, and pieces of the radioactive material were even passed around as curiosities. Some people used the glowing cesium to decorate their homes, while others applied it to their bodies, believing it to be a valuable or magical substance. This casual handling of the radioactive material led to widespread contamination in the community.

The Spread of Contamination

As the cesium-137 source was passed from person to person and place to place, the radioactive contamination spread rapidly throughout Goiânia. The contamination affected multiple locations, including homes, streets, and even public transportation. The radioactive material was carried on people's clothing, skin, and belongings, leading to a complex and challenging situation for authorities once the contamination was eventually discovered.

The initial symptoms of radiation exposure began to appear in those who had come into direct contact with the cesium. These symptoms included nausea, vomiting, diarrhea, skin burns, and hair loss—common indicators of acute radiation sickness. However, because radiation exposure was not initially suspected, the affected individuals did not receive appropriate medical attention, and the source of their illness remained unidentified.

The situation took a tragic turn when, on September 28, 1987, nearly two weeks after the cesium-137 source was first discovered, the contamination was finally recognized for what it was. The revelation came when one of the victims, Leide das Neves Ferreira, a 6-year-old girl who had played with the cesium-137 powder, was taken to a hospital with severe radiation burns. The doctors, suspecting that her condition might be related to radiation exposure, contacted the authorities, leading to the involvement of the National Nuclear Energy Commission (CNEN) and the immediate launch of a full-scale investigation.

Emergency Response and Containment Efforts

Once the nature of the disaster became clear, a massive emergency response was mobilized to contain the contamination and prevent further harm. The Brazilian government, with the assistance of the

International Atomic Energy Agency (IAEA), initiated a series of urgent actions to decontaminate affected areas, treat the victims, and manage the widespread panic that had gripped the city.

- **Identification and Isolation of Contaminated Sites:** The first priority for the authorities was to identify all the locations that had been contaminated by the cesium-137 source. This task was complicated by the fact that the radioactive material had been widely dispersed across the city. Teams of radiation experts were deployed to survey homes, streets, public buildings, and even vehicles. Using radiation detection equipment, they were able to map out the extent of the contamination and determine which areas required immediate intervention.

- **Decontamination Operations:** Once contaminated sites were identified, decontamination operations began. This process involved the removal and disposal of contaminated soil, debris, and personal belongings. In some cases, entire buildings had to be demolished to ensure that all traces of radiation were eliminated. Contaminated materials were carefully collected, sealed in lead-lined containers, and transported to secure disposal sites. The decontamination process was labor-intensive, costly, and required the expertise of specialists to ensure that all radioactive material was properly contained.

- **Medical Treatment for Radiation Exposure:** The victims of the Goiânia accident were treated at local hospitals, where they received care for their radiation-related injuries. Those who had been exposed to the highest levels of radiation, including the two original scavengers and their families, required intensive medical treatment. This included the administration of Prussian blue, a compound that helps reduce the absorption of cesium-137 in the body, and extensive wound care for radiation burns. Despite these efforts, four people ultimately died from radiation exposure, including 6-year-old Leide das Neves Ferreira.

- **Public Communication and Education:** In addition to the physical response, the Brazilian government faced the challenge of managing public fear and misinformation. Many residents of Goiânia were terrified of radiation, and rumors about the dangers of contamination spread quickly. Authorities worked to provide accurate information about the risks, the steps being taken to address the situation, and the measures people could take to protect themselves. Public education campaigns were launched to raise awareness about radiation safety and the importance of not handling unknown or potentially hazardous materials.

Long-Term Consequences of the Goiânia Accident

The Goiânia accident had far-reaching and long-lasting consequences, both for the affected community and for Brazil as a whole. The event exposed significant gaps in the country's regulatory framework for managing radioactive materials and prompted widespread changes in how such materials were handled, stored, and disposed of.

- **Health Impacts:** In addition to the immediate fatalities, many people who were exposed to radiation during the accident suffered long-term health effects. These included an increased risk of cancer, chronic health problems related to radiation exposure, and psychological trauma. The accident also had a profound impact on the mental health of the survivors and the broader community, with many people experiencing anxiety, depression, and social stigma as a result of their exposure.

- **Environmental Impact:** The environmental impact of the Goiânia accident was severe, with widespread contamination of soil, water, and buildings. The decontamination process removed much of the radioactive material, but the affected areas remained uninhabitable for years. The long-term environmental monitoring of these sites was necessary to ensure that no residual contamination posed a risk to human health or the environment.

- **Economic and Social Impact:** The economic impact of the Goiânia accident was significant, with the cost of the decontamination, medical treatment, and compensation for the victims running into millions of dollars. The event also had a profound social impact, particularly on those directly affected by the contamination. Many families were displaced, losing their homes and possessions to the decontamination process. Additionally, the social stigma attached to those who had been exposed to radiation led to discrimination and exclusion from their communities.

- **Regulatory Changes and Lessons Learned:** In the wake of the Goiânia accident, Brazil undertook a comprehensive review of its regulations and practices related to the handling of radioactive materials. The incident revealed the dangers of leaving radioactive sources unsecured and highlighted the need for stricter oversight and enforcement of safety standards. New regulations were introduced to ensure that all radioactive materials, particularly those in medical and industrial settings, were properly accounted for, securely stored, and safely disposed of at the end of their useful life. The Goiânia disaster also served as a wake-up call for the international community. It underscored the importance of global cooperation in managing the risks associated with radioactive materials and led to increased efforts to strengthen international standards and protocols for radiation safety.

Legacy and Memory of the Goiânia Accident

The Goiânia accident remains a poignant and tragic chapter in Brazil's history. It is remembered not only for the suffering and loss it caused but also for the lessons it imparted about the dangers of radioactive materials and the importance of vigilance in their management. The site of the accident has been transformed into a memorial to honor the victims and to serve as a reminder of the consequences of complacency and neglect.

For the people of Goiânia, the legacy of the disaster continues to shape their lives. The accident left a lasting mark on the community, both physically and emotionally. The trauma of the event, the loss of loved ones, and the social and economic upheaval it caused have had enduring effects on the survivors and their descendants.

In the broader context, the Goiânia accident serves as a case study in radiological emergency response, public health, and environmental management. It has been extensively studied by scientists, health professionals, and policymakers around the world, contributing to a deeper understanding of the complexities of managing radiological incidents and the importance of preparedness, education, and regulatory oversight.

Chapter 9: SL-1 Reactor Meltdown

The SL-1 reactor meltdown, officially known as the Stationary Low-Power Reactor Number One (SL-1) accident, represents one of the most tragic and significant nuclear incidents in the history of the United States. Occurring on January 3, 1961, at the National Reactor Testing Station (NRTS) in Idaho, this accident resulted in the first fatal nuclear reactor accident in the United States, claiming the lives of three military personnel and leaving an indelible mark on the history of nuclear energy and safety practices.

The SL-1 accident is a stark reminder of the potential dangers inherent in nuclear technology, particularly when safety protocols are not meticulously followed. It underscores the importance of stringent safety measures, rigorous training, and a thorough understanding of nuclear reactor operations. The incident also had far-reaching implications for the future of nuclear power in the United States, influencing reactor design, safety regulations, and emergency response protocols.

Background of the SL-1 Reactor

The SL-1 reactor was a small, experimental nuclear reactor designed for use in remote locations, such as Arctic outposts or isolated military bases. It was part of the Army Nuclear Power Program, which aimed to develop portable reactors capable of providing reliable power to military installations in remote or challenging environments. The SL-1 reactor, a boiling water reactor (BWR), was relatively simple in design, with a power output of just 3 megawatts (thermal), enough to generate electricity and heat for a small facility.

Constructed in the late 1950s, the SL-1 reactor was intended as a prototype for future reactors that could be deployed to remote locations where conventional power sources were unavailable or impractical. The reactor was operated by a team of military personnel, trained to manage the reactor's operations and ensure its safe functioning. The reactor core contained highly enriched uranium fuel, which, when bombarded with neutrons, would sustain a controlled nuclear fission reaction, producing heat to generate steam and electricity.

The Accident: Events Leading Up to the Meltdown

The SL-1 reactor accident occurred during a routine maintenance procedure on the evening of January 3, 1961. The reactor had been shut down for the holiday season, and the maintenance crew was tasked with preparing it for startup. The team consisted of three men: Army Specialists Richard L. McKinley and John A. Byrnes, and Navy Electrician's Mate Richard C. Legg. These men were experienced reactor operators, trained to handle the intricacies of the reactor's operation and maintenance.

The procedure that the crew was performing involved manually withdrawing a central control rod from the reactor core. Control rods are critical components in a nuclear reactor, as they absorb neutrons and regulate the rate of the fission reaction. By moving the control rods in and out of the reactor core, operators can control the reactor's power output. In this case, the central control rod was particularly important because it had the greatest impact on the reactor's reactivity.

The exact sequence of events that led to the accident remains somewhat unclear, as all three men present in the reactor control room perished in the explosion. However, investigators later determined that the central control rod was withdrawn too quickly and too far, causing the reactor to become supercritical. In other words, the reactor's fission reaction rapidly accelerated, producing an enormous amount of energy in a fraction of a second.

The Explosion and Its Immediate Aftermath

The rapid withdrawal of the central control rod triggered a sudden and catastrophic power excursion, where the reactor's power output spiked to an estimated 20,000 megawatts, far beyond its design capacity. The resulting energy release was so intense that it caused a violent steam explosion, which blasted the reactor vessel upward and propelled parts of the reactor and its components into the air. The explosion also released a significant amount of radioactive material into the reactor building.

Tragically, the three men in the control room were killed instantly by the explosion. Richard C. Legg was impaled by a piece of the reactor vessel and pinned to the ceiling of the control room, while John A. Byrnes and Richard L. McKinley suffered fatal injuries from the blast and the intense radiation. The explosion was so powerful that it not only destroyed much of the reactor but also caused severe structural damage to the reactor building.

The accident was not immediately discovered. When the crew failed to check in at the scheduled time, a rescue team was dispatched to the site. Upon arrival, they found the reactor building in disarray, with debris scattered and a thick cloud of radioactive steam and smoke filling the air. The rescue team, unaware of the severity of the radiation hazard, entered the building and discovered the bodies of the three men. Radiation levels inside the building were extremely high, posing a significant risk to the rescue workers.

The Response and Cleanup Efforts

The SL-1 accident triggered an immediate and extensive response from the Atomic Energy Commission (AEC), the military, and other federal agencies. The first priority was to secure the site and prevent further radioactive contamination. The reactor building was sealed off, and strict access controls were implemented to minimize the risk to personnel. Radiation monitoring teams were deployed to assess the extent of contamination and to establish safe zones around the reactor site.

- **Radiation Exposure and Health Risks:** The high radiation levels at the site posed serious health risks to those involved in the initial response and cleanup efforts. The bodies of the three men had to be recovered and removed under extremely hazardous conditions, with rescue workers wearing protective gear to shield themselves from radiation. The workers involved in the cleanup were subjected to strict radiation exposure limits, and their health was closely monitored throughout the operation.
- **Decontamination and Reactor Dismantling:** The cleanup of the SL-1 site was a complex and lengthy process. The reactor had to be carefully dismantled, and the radioactive debris was removed and safely stored. The reactor building was decontaminated as much as possible, although some areas remained highly radioactive and had to be sealed off permanently. The contaminated materials were transported to secure disposal sites, and the entire area around the reactor was subjected to thorough radiation surveys to ensure that no residual contamination remained.
- **Investigation and Analysis:** In the wake of the accident, a thorough investigation was launched to determine the cause of the reactor meltdown and to identify any lessons that could be learned to prevent future incidents. The investigation involved a detailed analysis of the reactor's design, the procedures followed by the crew, and the sequence of events leading up to the accident. While the exact circumstances of the control rod withdrawal could not be conclusively

determined, it was clear that human error played a significant role in the accident. The investigation also examined the design and safety features of the SL-1 reactor. It was found that the reactor's design had several vulnerabilities, including the potential for a single control rod to cause a rapid and uncontrollable power excursion if withdrawn too far. The accident highlighted the need for more robust safety systems, including automatic shutdown mechanisms and more rigorous operator training programs.

Long-Term Consequences of the SL-1 Accident

The SL-1 reactor meltdown had profound and far-reaching consequences for the nuclear industry, particularly in the United States. The accident prompted a reevaluation of reactor safety standards and led to significant changes in the design, operation, and regulation of nuclear reactors.

- **Impact on Reactor Design:** One of the most significant outcomes of the SL-1 accident was the recognition of the need for more stringent safety features in reactor design. Subsequent reactor designs incorporated redundant safety systems to prevent a single point of failure from leading to a catastrophic accident. This included the implementation of more sophisticated control rod mechanisms, automatic shutdown systems, and enhanced monitoring and alarm systems to detect and respond to abnormal conditions.

- **Regulatory Reforms:** The SL-1 accident also led to reforms in the regulatory framework governing nuclear reactors in the United States. The Atomic Energy Commission (AEC) introduced stricter regulations and oversight for reactor operations, including more rigorous safety inspections and operator certification requirements. These reforms were aimed at ensuring that all nuclear reactors operated with the highest levels of safety and that operators were fully trained and prepared to handle any potential emergencies.

- **Impact on Nuclear Policy:** The SL-1 accident had a lasting impact on public perception of nuclear power and influenced nuclear policy in the United States. The incident raised awareness of the potential risks associated with nuclear reactors, particularly those in remote or military locations. It also contributed to growing public concern about the safety of nuclear power, leading to increased scrutiny of nuclear energy programs and influencing the direction of future nuclear policy.
- **Legacy and Lessons Learned:** The legacy of the SL-1 accident is reflected in the lessons learned from the tragedy. The accident underscored the importance of human factors in reactor safety, particularly the need for rigorous training and adherence to safety protocols. It also highlighted the potential consequences of design flaws and the need for continuous improvement in reactor safety technology. The SL-1 reactor meltdown remains a sobering reminder of the dangers associated with nuclear technology and the critical importance of safety in its application. The incident has been extensively studied by nuclear engineers, safety experts, and historians, and it continues to serve as a case study in the complexities of nuclear reactor operations and the challenges of ensuring nuclear safety.

Chapter 10: Hiroshima Incident

The Hiroshima Incident, one of the most profound and devastating events in human history, occurred on August 6, 1945, during the final stages of World War II. On this day, the United States dropped an atomic bomb on the Japanese city of Hiroshima, marking the first time a nuclear weapon was used in warfare. The bomb, codenamed "Little Boy," unleashed unprecedented destruction and ushered in the nuclear age, forever altering the course of global history. The Hiroshima Incident is not only a pivotal moment in the annals of war but also a stark reminder of the catastrophic potential of nuclear weapons.

This tragic event resulted in the immediate deaths of tens of thousands of people, with many more suffering from injuries and radiation sickness in the aftermath. The city of Hiroshima was almost entirely obliterated, and the psychological and environmental impacts of the bombing have resonated for generations. The incident remains a powerful symbol of the horrors of nuclear warfare and serves as a cautionary tale about the consequences of using such destructive technology.

The Prelude to the Hiroshima Bombing

The decision to use atomic bombs on Japan was shaped by a complex interplay of military strategy, geopolitical considerations, and scientific advancements. By 1945, World War II had raged for nearly six years, with the Axis powers, including Germany and Japan, fighting against the Allies, which included the United States, the United Kingdom, the Soviet Union, and China, among others. The war in Europe had ended in May 1945 with the defeat of Nazi Germany, but the conflict in the Pacific continued, with Japan refusing to surrender despite suffering significant military defeats and the loss of key territories.

The United States, under President Harry S. Truman, sought a way to bring the war to a swift conclusion while minimizing further Allied casualties. The Japanese military had demonstrated a willingness to fight to the bitter end, as seen in the fierce battles of Iwo Jima and Okinawa, where both sides suffered heavy losses. The prospect of a costly invasion of the Japanese home islands loomed large, and estimates of potential Allied casualties ranged from hundreds of thousands to millions.

Amidst this backdrop, the Manhattan Project, a top-secret research and development program, had successfully developed the world's first atomic bombs. Led by physicist J. Robert Oppenheimer and involving some of the brightest minds in science, the Manhattan Project culminated in the testing of the first atomic bomb, codenamed "Trinity," in the New Mexico desert on July 16, 1945. The successful test confirmed the feasibility of using nuclear weapons in combat, presenting the United States with a powerful, yet morally complex, option to force Japan's surrender.

The decision to drop the bomb on Hiroshima was made after intense deliberation among U.S. military and political leaders. They considered various factors, including the potential to save lives by avoiding a prolonged war, the desire to demonstrate the bomb's destructive power to the world (particularly to the Soviet Union), and the hope that such an overwhelming display of force would compel Japan to surrender unconditionally. Hiroshima, a city of strategic military importance and a population of approximately 350,000, was selected as the first target.

The Day of the Bombing: August 6, 1945

On the morning of August 6, 1945, at 8:15 a.m. local time, the B-29 bomber *Enola Gay*, piloted by Colonel Paul W. Tibbets, released the atomic bomb "Little Boy" over Hiroshima. The bomb detonated approximately 600 meters (1,968 feet) above the ground, creating a massive explosion equivalent to about 15 kilotons of TNT. The detonation produced a blinding flash of light, followed by a wave of intense heat and a powerful shockwave that leveled buildings and incinerated everything in its immediate vicinity.

The impact of the explosion was catastrophic. The center of Hiroshima was reduced to rubble, with an estimated radius of total destruction extending more than a mile from the hypocenter. Temperatures at the core of the explosion soared to several million degrees Celsius, causing instant vaporization of everything near the blast. The intense heat ignited fires across the city, creating a firestorm that further exacerbated the destruction.

- **Immediate Casualties and Devastation:** The initial blast killed an estimated 70,000 to 80,000 people instantly, with thousands more suffering horrific injuries from the heat and flying debris. Those closer to the hypocenter experienced instant death or severe burns, while those farther away were injured by collapsing buildings, shrapnel, and radiation exposure. Many survivors, known as *hibakusha* (literally "explosion-affected people"), would endure lifelong physical and psychological scars from the event. The destruction extended far beyond the immediate casualties. Hiroshima's infrastructure, including homes, schools, hospitals, and factories, was obliterated. The city's water supply was disrupted, fires raged uncontrolled, and the survivors faced an immediate humanitarian crisis with limited medical care, food, and shelter. The sheer scale of the devastation overwhelmed the city's ability to respond, and the aftermath was marked by chaos, suffering, and death.
- **Radiation and Long-Term Effects:** One of the most insidious and long-lasting consequences of the Hiroshima bombing was the exposure to radiation. The bomb released

a significant amount of ionizing radiation, which spread throughout the city and affected those who survived the initial blast. Many survivors experienced acute radiation sickness, characterized by symptoms such as nausea, vomiting, hair loss, and bleeding. In the weeks and months following the bombing, radiation-related deaths increased, bringing the total death toll by the end of 1945 to an estimated 140,000 people. The long-term effects of radiation exposure continued to manifest for years and decades after the bombing. Survivors suffered from an increased risk of cancer, particularly leukemia, as well as other health problems such as cataracts, infertility, and chronic illnesses. Children exposed to radiation in utero were born with a higher incidence of birth defects and developmental issues. The psychological trauma endured by the survivors also had a profound impact, with many experiencing post-traumatic stress disorder (PTSD), depression, and anxiety.

The Immediate Aftermath: Japan's Response and Surrender

In the days following the bombing of Hiroshima, the full extent of the destruction became increasingly apparent. The Japanese government, initially uncertain of what had happened, soon realized that a new and devastating weapon had been used against them. Despite the horrific loss of life in Hiroshima, Japan did not immediately surrender. The country's leadership was divided, with some military officials advocating for continued resistance, while others recognized the futility of further conflict.

On August 9, 1945, just three days after the Hiroshima bombing, the United States dropped a second atomic bomb on the city of Nagasaki. This second bombing, coupled with the Soviet Union's declaration of war against Japan and the invasion of Japanese-held territories in

Manchuria, led to the collapse of Japanese resolve. On August 15, 1945, Emperor Hirohito announced Japan's unconditional surrender in a radio address to the nation, marking the end of World War II.

Global Reaction and the Ethical Debate

The Hiroshima Incident immediately reverberated around the world, shocking global leaders, military officials, and civilians alike. The unprecedented destruction caused by the atomic bomb raised profound ethical questions about the use of nuclear weapons, the morality of targeting civilian populations, and the implications for future warfare. While some argued that the bombings were necessary to end the war quickly and save lives, others condemned the use of such a devastating weapon as inhumane and unnecessary.

- **Ethical and Moral Considerations:** The decision to use atomic bombs against Japan remains one of the most controversial in history. Proponents of the decision argued that the bombings forced Japan to surrender, thereby avoiding a costly invasion of the Japanese mainland and potentially saving hundreds of thousands of lives, both Allied and Japanese. They also pointed to Japan's wartime atrocities, such as the attack on Pearl Harbor and the brutal treatment of prisoners of war, as justification for using the bomb to bring a swift end to the conflict. Critics, however, contended that Japan was already on the brink of surrender and that the use of atomic bombs was unnecessary and disproportionate. They argued that the bombings targeted civilian populations, causing immense suffering and setting a dangerous precedent for future conflicts. The ethical debate over Hiroshima has continued to this day, with historians, ethicists, and policymakers grappling with the moral implications of nuclear warfare.

- **Impact on International Relations and Nuclear Policy:** The Hiroshima Incident had profound implications for international relations and the development of nuclear policy in the post-war world. The bombings of Hiroshima and Nagasaki demonstrated the devastating power of nuclear weapons, leading to a global recognition of the need to control and regulate their use. In the years following World War II, the United States and the Soviet Union embarked on a nuclear arms race, developing increasingly powerful and sophisticated weapons that posed an existential threat to humanity. The Cold War era was marked by a delicate balance of power, with the concept of mutually assured destruction (MAD) serving as a deterrent to the use of nuclear weapons. The horrors of Hiroshima also spurred efforts to prevent the proliferation of nuclear weapons, leading to the establishment of international treaties and organizations aimed at controlling nuclear technology and promoting disarmament. The Treaty on the Non-Proliferation of Nuclear Weapons (NPT), signed in 1968, remains a cornerstone of global efforts to prevent the spread of nuclear weapons and promote peaceful uses of nuclear energy.

Legacy of the Hiroshima Incident

The legacy of the Hiroshima Incident is multifaceted, encompassing the immediate human toll, the long-term health and environmental consequences, the ethical and moral debates, and the impact on global nuclear policy. Hiroshima has become a symbol of the destructive power of nuclear weapons and a focal point for efforts to promote peace and prevent future nuclear conflicts.

- **Hiroshima Peace Memorial and Advocacy for Nuclear Disarmament:** In the years following the bombing,

Hiroshima transformed from a city of devastation to a city of peace. The Hiroshima Peace Memorial Park, established in 1954, serves as a poignant reminder of the tragedy and a place for reflection and remembrance. The park includes the Hiroshima Peace Memorial (commonly known as the Atomic Bomb Dome), which stands as a stark symbol of the destruction, and the Hiroshima Peace Memorial Museum, which educates visitors about the events of August 6, 1945, and the broader implications of nuclear warfare. Hiroshima's role as a center for peace advocacy has grown over the decades, with the city hosting annual memorial ceremonies on August 6 to honor the victims and call for the abolition of nuclear weapons. Survivors of the bombing, known as *hibakusha*, have played a crucial role in these efforts, sharing their experiences and advocating for a world free of nuclear weapons. Their testimonies have been instrumental in raising awareness of the human cost of nuclear warfare and in building global support for disarmament initiatives.

- **Cultural and Educational Impact:** The Hiroshima Incident has also left an indelible mark on culture, literature, film, and education. The bombing has been the subject of countless books, films, and documentaries that explore the event from various perspectives, including the experiences of survivors, the decision-making process behind the bombings, and the broader implications for humanity. Works such as John Hersey's *Hiroshima*, a groundbreaking report on the experiences of six survivors, and the films *Barefoot Gen* and *Grave of the Fireflies*, have brought the human stories of Hiroshima to a global audience, fostering empathy and understanding. Educational initiatives around the world have incorporated the Hiroshima Incident into curricula, using it as a case study to discuss the ethics of war, the dangers of nuclear weapons, and the importance of peacebuilding. The lessons of Hiroshima continue to resonate with new generations, reminding them of the consequences of war and the need to strive for a more peaceful and just world.

Chapter 11: Nagasaki Incident

The Nagasaki Incident, one of the most pivotal and catastrophic events in modern history, occurred on August 9, 1945, just three days after the atomic bombing of Hiroshima. This event marked the second and, to date, the last use of a nuclear weapon in warfare. The United States dropped an atomic bomb on the Japanese city of Nagasaki, resulting in widespread destruction and loss of life. The bomb, codenamed "Fat Man," had a slightly different design and was more powerful than the "Little Boy" bomb dropped on Hiroshima. The Nagasaki Incident played a critical role in Japan's decision to surrender, effectively bringing World War II to a close. However, the human, environmental, and moral consequences of this event have reverberated through the decades, making it a subject of intense study, reflection, and debate.

The Nagasaki bombing was not just an isolated military action but a significant event that influenced international relations, nuclear policy, and the global understanding of the devastating impact of nuclear warfare. It serves as a stark reminder of the destructive potential of nuclear weapons and the need for ongoing efforts toward disarmament and peace.

Context and Prelude to the Nagasaki Bombing

The Nagasaki Incident cannot be fully understood without considering the broader context of World War II, particularly the final stages of the Pacific War. By 1945, the Allied forces had made significant advances against the Axis powers. Germany had already surrendered in May, but Japan continued to resist, even in the face of overwhelming odds. The Japanese military leadership was determined to fight to the end, adhering to the Bushido code, which emphasized honor and the willingness to die rather than surrender.

The United States, under the leadership of President Harry S. Truman, sought a means to force Japan's unconditional surrender without incurring the massive casualties expected from a conventional invasion of the Japanese home islands. The battles of Iwo Jima and Okinawa had demonstrated the high cost of such operations, with tens of thousands of American and Japanese lives lost. The alternative, as presented by the newly developed atomic bombs, was seen as a way to end the war quickly and decisively.

The decision to use atomic bombs was also influenced by geopolitical considerations, particularly the desire to demonstrate American military superiority to the Soviet Union, which was emerging as a post-war rival. The Manhattan Project, the secret U.S. program to develop atomic weapons, had succeeded in producing two types of bombs: a uranium-based bomb (Little Boy) and a plutonium-based bomb (Fat Man). The successful detonation of an atomic bomb in the Trinity test on July 16, 1945, in New Mexico, provided the final proof that these weapons could be used effectively in combat.

Hiroshima was the first target, bombed on August 6, 1945, causing unprecedented devastation and killing tens of thousands of people instantly. However, Japan did not immediately surrender, and the U.S. military prepared to drop a second bomb to further pressure the Japanese government.

Nagasaki as a Target

Nagasaki was not the primary target for the second atomic bomb. The original target was the city of Kokura, an important industrial and military center. However, on the day of the bombing, August 9, 1945, Kokura was obscured by clouds, smoke, and haze, making it difficult for the bomber crew to visually confirm the target as required by their orders. After three unsuccessful passes over Kokura, the B-29 bomber, named Bockscar and piloted by Major Charles W. Sweeney, diverted to the secondary target: Nagasaki.

Nagasaki, located on the western coast of Kyushu, Japan's southernmost main island, was a major port city with significant industrial facilities, including shipyards, steel mills, and arms factories. It had been a key center for Japan's military production during the war. The city's unique geography, with its hilly terrain and deep harbor, provided some natural protection from conventional bombing, but it was not immune to the destructive power of an atomic bomb.

Nagasaki's population at the time of the bombing was estimated to be around 240,000, though this number fluctuated due to wartime evacuations and the presence of workers brought in to support the war effort. The city was a mix of industrial areas and residential neighborhoods, with some parts of the city densely populated.

The Day of the Bombing: August 9, 1945

On the morning of August 9, 1945, at approximately 11:02 a.m. local time, the Bockscar dropped the "Fat Man" bomb over Nagasaki. Unlike the uranium-based Little Boy, Fat Man was a plutonium implosion-type bomb with an explosive yield of about 21 kilotons, significantly more powerful than the bomb dropped on Hiroshima.

- **The Bomb's Impact:** The bomb exploded about 500 meters (1,650 feet) above Nagasaki, near the district of Urakami, which was home to a large Catholic community and several important factories. The explosion created a fireball with temperatures estimated to reach several million degrees Celsius at its center, incinerating everything within a 1,000-meter radius. The intense heat caused flash burns to people and objects within several kilometers of the hypocenter. The terrain of Nagasaki, with its hills and valleys, somewhat limited the extent of the blast compared to the flatter city of Hiroshima, but the destruction was still immense. The blast and subsequent firestorm destroyed or severely damaged over 40% of the city's buildings, including homes, factories, schools, and hospitals. The industrial heart of the city was devastated, with the Mitsubishi Steel and Arms Works and the Mitsubishi Electric Works suffering severe damage.

- **Immediate Casualties and Devastation:** The immediate death toll from the Nagasaki bombing is estimated to be between 40,000 and 75,000 people, with a significant number of those deaths occurring instantaneously from the blast and intense heat. Thousands more were injured, many of whom would later die from their injuries and radiation sickness. As with Hiroshima, the actual number of casualties has been difficult to determine due to the chaotic conditions following the bombing and the destruction of records. Those who survived the initial blast faced horrific conditions. Many suffered from severe burns, traumatic injuries, and radiation sickness, which manifested in symptoms such as nausea, vomiting, hair loss, and hemorrhaging. The medical facilities in Nagasaki were overwhelmed, with many doctors and nurses among the casualties, and there was a severe shortage of supplies and equipment to treat the wounded.

- **Radiation and Long-Term Health Effects:** One of the most significant and long-lasting impacts of the Nagasaki bombing was the exposure to ionizing radiation. Survivors of the bombing, known as *hibakusha*, were exposed to high levels of radiation, leading to acute radiation sickness in the days and weeks following the explosion. Radiation exposure also had long-term health consequences, including an increased incidence of leukemia and other cancers, as well as chronic illnesses and genetic damage that affected subsequent generations. In the years following the bombing, many survivors suffered from the lingering effects of radiation exposure, including weakened immune systems, chronic pain, and psychological trauma. The stigma associated with being a hibakusha also led to social and economic discrimination, as survivors were often ostracized and faced difficulties in finding employment or marriage partners due to fears of radiation-related health problems.

Japan's Response and the Path to Surrender

The bombing of Nagasaki, coming just three days after the Hiroshima bombing, placed immense pressure on the Japanese government to surrender. The sheer scale of the destruction, combined with the threat of additional atomic bombings and the Soviet Union's entry into the war against Japan on August 8, 1945, convinced many Japanese leaders that continuing the war was futile.

Emperor Hirohito, who had been considering surrender but faced opposition from some military leaders, ultimately decided that the only way to prevent further suffering and the potential annihilation of Japan was to accept the terms of the Allies' Potsdam Declaration. On August 15, 1945, Emperor Hirohito announced Japan's unconditional surrender in a radio broadcast, bringing an end to World War II. This broadcast, known as the Gyokuon-hōsō (Jewel Voice Broadcast), was the first time the Japanese public had heard the Emperor's voice, and it marked a profound moment in Japanese history.

The surrender of Japan was formalized on September 2, 1945, with the signing of the Instrument of Surrender aboard the USS Missouri in Tokyo Bay. This event marked the official end of World War II, but it also signaled the beginning of a new era of global politics, characterized by the Cold War and the nuclear arms race.

The Global Reaction and Ethical Debates

The Nagasaki Incident, like the Hiroshima bombing, sparked immediate and intense global reactions. The use of atomic bombs against civilian populations was unprecedented, and the scale of the destruction shocked the world. The bombings of Hiroshima and Nagasaki have since been the subject of extensive ethical and moral debate, with historians, ethicists, and policymakers grappling with the implications of using such weapons.

- **Ethical and Moral Considerations:** The ethical debate surrounding the Nagasaki bombing, and the use of atomic bombs in general, centers on several key issues. Proponents of the bombings argue that they were necessary to end the war quickly and save lives by avoiding a prolonged conflict and potential invasion of Japan. They contend that the bombings forced Japan to surrender, thereby preventing further loss of life on both sides. However, critics argue that the bombings were unnecessary and inhumane, as Japan was already on the brink of surrender and the use of such devastating weapons on civilian populations violated ethical principles. The fact that Nagasaki was bombed just three days after Hiroshima, before Japan had a chance to fully comprehend and respond to the first bombing, has also been criticized as overly hasty and disproportionate.
- **Impact on Nuclear Policy and Arms Control:** The Nagasaki Incident played a significant role in shaping post-war nuclear policy and the global approach to arms control. The sheer destructive power of atomic bombs, as demonstrated in Hiroshima and Nagasaki, led to widespread fear of nuclear warfare and sparked efforts to control and eventually eliminate nuclear weapons. In the immediate aftermath of the war, the United States enjoyed a monopoly on nuclear

weapons, but this advantage was short-lived. The Soviet Union successfully tested its first atomic bomb in 1949, leading to an arms race between the two superpowers that would define the Cold War era. The development of more powerful thermonuclear weapons, or hydrogen bombs, in the 1950s further heightened the stakes, leading to the doctrine of Mutually Assured Destruction (MAD), where both the U.S. and the Soviet Union possessed the capability to annihilate each other in the event of a nuclear conflict.

- **Efforts Toward Disarmament and Peace:** The horrors of Hiroshima and Nagasaki also gave rise to a global movement for nuclear disarmament. Organizations such as the United Nations and various non-governmental groups have worked tirelessly to promote arms control treaties, reduce nuclear stockpiles, and prevent the spread of nuclear weapons. Landmark treaties such as the Nuclear Non-Proliferation Treaty (NPT) of 1968 and the Comprehensive Nuclear-Test-Ban Treaty (CTBT) of 1996 have been key components of these efforts. Nagasaki, like Hiroshima, has become a symbol of peace and a focal point for disarmament advocacy. The city hosts annual memorial ceremonies on August 9 to honor the victims of the bombing and to call for the abolition of nuclear weapons. Survivors of the bombing, along with political leaders and peace activists, continue to use Nagasaki as a platform to promote a world free of nuclear weapons.

Nagasaki's Recovery and Legacy

In the years following the bombing, Nagasaki, like Hiroshima, faced the daunting task of rebuilding from the ruins. The city's recovery was a long and challenging process, complicated by the physical destruction, the health impacts of radiation exposure, and the psychological trauma experienced by survivors.

- **Reconstruction and Memorialization:** The reconstruction of Nagasaki began in the immediate aftermath of the bombing, with a focus on rebuilding infrastructure, housing, and industry. Over time, the city was able to restore much of its economic base, though the loss of life and the destruction of key industrial facilities left lasting scars. The rebuilding process also included the establishment of memorials and museums to preserve the memory of the bombing and educate future generations about its significance. One of the most important memorials in Nagasaki is the Nagasaki Peace Park, established near the hypocenter of the blast. The park includes several monuments, including the famous Peace Statue, a large bronze figure that symbolizes the city's desire for peace and the abolition of nuclear weapons. The Nagasaki Atomic Bomb Museum, located nearby, provides a comprehensive account of the bombing, its aftermath, and the broader context of nuclear warfare.

- **Nagasaki as a Center for Peace Advocacy:** Like Hiroshima, Nagasaki has become a global center for peace advocacy and education. The city's leaders and citizens have been at the forefront of efforts to promote nuclear disarmament and to ensure that the lessons of the bombing are not forgotten. Nagasaki's commitment to peace is reflected in its participation in international initiatives such as Mayors for Peace, a global organization that works to promote the abolition of nuclear weapons and to foster a culture of peace. Survivors of the Nagasaki bombing, or *hibakusha*, have played a crucial role in these efforts, sharing their experiences with audiences around the world and advocating for a future without nuclear weapons. Their testimonies, along with the continued research into the health and environmental impacts of the bombing, have provided valuable insights into the long-term consequences of nuclear warfare.

Chapter 12: Thule Air Base B-52 Crash

The Thule Air Base B-52 crash, also known as the Thule incident, is a significant event in Cold War history. It occurred on January 21, 1968, when a U.S. Air Force B-52G Stratofortress, carrying four hydrogen bombs, crashed near Thule Air Base in Greenland. The incident is notable not only for the crash itself but also for its implications on U.S. military operations, nuclear weapons policy, and international relations during a period of heightened tension between the United States and the Soviet Union.

Background and Context

The Thule Air Base is a U.S. military installation located in the northwest of Greenland, strategically positioned near the Arctic Circle. Established during World War II, it became a critical part of the United States' defense network during the Cold War, particularly in the context of monitoring Soviet missile activity. The base was equipped with radar systems that could detect incoming ballistic missiles, making it a key element in the U.S. early warning system.

During the Cold War, the United States adopted a policy known as "Operation Chrome Dome," which involved the continuous airborne alert of nuclear-armed B-52 bombers. These bombers were kept in the air 24/7 to ensure a rapid retaliatory capability in the event of a Soviet first strike. The bombers were equipped with hydrogen bombs, and their flight routes often took them near or over the Arctic region, close to the Soviet Union. The Thule Air Base served as a critical waypoint for these missions, providing support and refueling services.

The Crash

On January 21, 1968, a B-52G Stratofortress was on a Chrome Dome mission, flying over the Arctic. The aircraft, designated "Buzz One

Four," was carrying four B28FI thermonuclear bombs. The crew consisted of seven members, including the pilot, co-pilot, and navigators. As the bomber approached Thule Air Base, a fire broke out in the navigator's compartment, likely due to a malfunctioning heating pad.

The fire quickly spread, filling the cockpit with smoke and causing the crew to lose control of the aircraft. The pilot attempted to divert the plane to Thule Air Base for an emergency landing, but the situation deteriorated rapidly. Realizing that the fire could not be contained and that the aircraft was no longer flyable, the crew was forced to abandon the plane.

Six of the seven crew members successfully ejected and were later rescued by search and rescue teams. Tragically, one crew member, Captain Leonard Svitenko, died as he was unable to escape the aircraft before it crashed. The B-52G, now completely out of control, crashed onto the sea ice of North Star Bay, approximately seven miles west of Thule Air Base. Upon impact, the conventional explosives in the bombers' nuclear weapons detonated, causing a massive explosion that scattered debris and radioactive material across the ice and into the surrounding environment.

Immediate Aftermath

The crash triggered a major crisis, both in terms of the potential environmental impact and the geopolitical ramifications. The U.S. military, in coordination with the Danish government (Greenland being an autonomous territory of Denmark), launched "Operation Crested Ice," a large-scale cleanup and recovery operation.

The primary concern was the recovery of the nuclear weapons and the containment of radioactive contamination. The conventional explosives in the bombs had detonated upon impact, but the nuclear cores did not achieve a full-scale nuclear detonation, which would have resulted in a catastrophic explosion. However, the crash still scattered plutonium and other radioactive materials across the crash site, contaminating the sea ice and the surrounding area.

Operation Crested Ice

Operation Crested Ice was one of the largest and most complex cleanup operations ever undertaken by the U.S. military. The operation involved hundreds of personnel, including military engineers, scientists, and technicians, who worked around the clock in the harsh Arctic conditions to recover the debris and decontaminate the site.

The first priority was to locate and recover the four nuclear bombs that had been on board the B-52. Due to the intensity of the explosion and the spread of debris, this was a challenging task. The search teams used a combination of aerial surveys, ground-penetrating radar, and other detection methods to locate the bomb fragments scattered across the ice and sea floor.

In addition to the recovery of the bombs, the operation also focused on the containment and cleanup of radioactive contamination. The sea ice and snow were heavily contaminated with plutonium, which posed a significant environmental and health risk. The contaminated ice and snow were removed and transported to the United States for proper disposal. Additionally, the seawater in North Star Bay was also contaminated, and measures were taken to monitor and mitigate the environmental impact.

Despite the harsh conditions and the complexity of the operation, the cleanup was largely successful. By September 1968, the majority of the debris and contaminated material had been removed, and the site was declared safe. However, the environmental impact of the crash continued to be a concern, and studies were conducted over the following decades to monitor the long-term effects of the incident.

Geopolitical Implications

The Thule Air Base B-52 crash had significant geopolitical implications, particularly in the context of U.S.-Danish relations and the broader Cold War dynamics. Greenland, while a territory of Denmark, had been leased to the United States for military purposes under the 1951 U.S.-Danish Defense Agreement. This agreement allowed the U.S. to operate military installations in Greenland, including Thule Air Base, but it also stipulated that Denmark's nuclear-free policy would be respected.

The crash revealed the presence of nuclear weapons in Greenland, which was a direct violation of Denmark's nuclear-free policy. This led to a major diplomatic crisis between Denmark and the United States. The Danish government was placed in a difficult position, as it had to balance its alliance with the United States against the strong anti-nuclear sentiment among the Danish public.

In the immediate aftermath of the crash, the Danish government sought to downplay the incident, but as more details emerged, public outcry grew. The Danish Prime Minister at the time, Jens Otto Krag, faced intense pressure from opposition parties and the media to address the issue. The U.S. government, for its part, sought to manage the situation by emphasizing the cleanup efforts and downplaying the extent of the contamination.

The Thule incident also had broader implications for U.S. nuclear policy and military operations. The crash highlighted the risks associated with the Chrome Dome missions and the potential for catastrophic accidents involving nuclear weapons. In the wake of the incident, the U.S. government faced increased scrutiny over its nuclear policies, both domestically and internationally.

The incident contributed to a growing debate within the U.S. government and military about the wisdom of maintaining continuous airborne alert missions. In 1968, just months after the Thule crash, the U.S. Air Force decided to end Operation Chrome Dome, citing the risks and costs associated with the program. The end of Chrome Dome marked a significant shift in U.S. nuclear strategy, as the focus shifted away from continuous airborne alert to other forms of nuclear deterrence, such as missile-based systems.

Environmental and Health Concerns

The environmental impact of the Thule crash has been a subject of ongoing concern and study. The explosion and subsequent cleanup operation left a significant amount of radioactive material in the environment, particularly plutonium, which has a half-life of 24,100 years and poses long-term risks to human health and the environment.

In the years following the crash, studies were conducted to assess the extent of contamination and its potential impact on the local population and the environment. These studies found elevated levels of plutonium in the ice and seawater around the crash site, as well as in the air and soil. The long-term health effects of this contamination, particularly on the local Inuit population, have been a source of concern.

In addition to the immediate cleanup efforts, the U.S. and Danish governments have conducted ongoing monitoring of the site to assess the long-term environmental impact. These studies have shown that while much of the contamination was removed during Operation Crested Ice, some residual contamination remains. The long-term impact of this contamination on the Arctic environment and the health of local communities remains a subject of study and debate.

Legal and Diplomatic Fallout

The Thule incident also had significant legal and diplomatic ramifications. In the years following the crash, a series of legal disputes and compensation claims arose, both from the Danish government and from individuals affected by the incident.

One of the most significant legal cases involved the workers who participated in the cleanup operation. Many of these workers later reported health problems that they attributed to their exposure to radioactive materials during the cleanup. These health issues included various forms of cancer, respiratory problems, and other illnesses. In the years following the incident, a group of these workers, known as the "Thule Workers," filed lawsuits against the U.S. government, seeking compensation for their health problems.

The legal battles over compensation for the Thule Workers continued for decades, with mixed results. In some cases, the workers were able to secure settlements or compensation, but in many cases, their claims were denied or dismissed. The issue of compensation for the Thule Workers remains a contentious and unresolved aspect of the incident.

In addition to the legal disputes, the Thule incident also had a lasting impact on U.S.-Danish relations. The Danish government, under pressure from its citizens, sought to renegotiate the terms of the U.S.-Danish Defense Agreement to ensure greater transparency and oversight of U.S. military activities in Greenland. This led to a series of diplomatic negotiations between the two countries, which ultimately resulted in changes to the agreement.

Legacy of the Thule Incident

The Thule Air Base B-52 crash remains one of the most significant and controversial incidents in the history of U.S. military operations during the Cold War. The incident highlighted the risks associated with the deployment and transport of nuclear weapons and led to significant changes in U.S. military policy and strategy.

In addition to its impact on U.S. military operations, the Thule incident also had a lasting impact on international relations and nuclear policy. The incident contributed to a growing awareness of the dangers of nuclear weapons and the need for greater oversight and control over their deployment. It also played a role in shaping the broader debate over nuclear disarmament and arms control during the Cold War.

The Thule incident also had a significant environmental legacy, with ongoing concerns about the impact of radioactive contamination in the Arctic region. The incident serves as a reminder of the long-term environmental and health risks associated with nuclear weapons and the need for continued vigilance in managing these risks.

Chapter 13: RTG Accidents

Radioisotope Thermoelectric Generators (RTGs) are compact, nuclear-powered devices that convert heat released by the decay of radioactive material into electricity. These devices have been widely used in situations where reliable, long-term power sources are needed, and solar power or batteries are impractical. RTGs have played a critical role in powering remote facilities, unmanned spacecraft, navigation beacons, and weather stations. However, despite their usefulness, RTGs have also been associated with a series of accidents, some of which have had serious consequences for human health and the environment.

The Technology Behind RTGs

RTGs work by harnessing the heat produced from the radioactive decay of isotopes like plutonium-238, strontium-90, or polonium-210. These isotopes are selected for their ability to emit significant amounts of heat over long periods. The heat is then converted into electricity using thermocouples, which exploit the Seebeck effect—a phenomenon where a voltage is generated across two dissimilar conductors that are subjected to a temperature difference.

Because RTGs do not have moving parts, they are highly reliable and can operate unattended for decades. This makes them ideal for powering devices in extreme environments, such as deep space missions where solar power is not feasible. However, the use of highly radioactive materials means that RTGs pose significant risks if they are damaged, improperly handled, or disposed of carelessly.

Historical Context: RTGs in Cold War-Era Applications

The use of RTGs dates back to the 1950s, during the height of the Cold War, when both the United States and the Soviet Union were exploring ways to power remote and inaccessible locations. The military applications of RTGs were particularly appealing because they could provide a consistent power source for espionage equipment, surveillance stations, and other critical infrastructure in areas far from the grid.

In addition to military uses, RTGs were deployed in civilian applications, such as lighthouses, meteorological stations, and space exploration missions. The Soviet Union, in particular, was known for its extensive use of RTGs in remote areas of Siberia and the Arctic, where the harsh climate made other power sources impractical.

Notable RTG Accidents: A Chronology of Tragedies

Over the decades, several accidents involving RTGs have been documented. These incidents highlight the potential dangers of RTGs and the catastrophic consequences that can arise from their mishandling or accidental damage.

- **The Kosmos 954 Incident (1978):** One of the most notorious RTG accidents occurred when the Soviet reconnaissance satellite Kosmos 954, equipped with a nuclear reactor, malfunctioned and re-entered the Earth's atmosphere. The satellite broke apart over Canada, scattering radioactive debris over a vast area. The RTG's nuclear material was dispersed, leading to a large-scale cleanup operation known as Operation Morning Light. The incident raised international concerns about the safety of nuclear-powered satellites and the potential for radioactive contamination.
- **The Georgia RTG Incident (2001-2002):** In the early 2000s, a series of RTG accidents in the country of Georgia highlighted the dangers of abandoned radioactive sources. During the collapse of the Soviet Union, many RTGs were left in remote areas without proper safeguards. In one instance, a group of woodcutters in the Georgian forest discovered an

abandoned RTG, unaware of its radioactive nature. Several individuals suffered severe radiation burns and acute radiation sickness after prolonged exposure. This incident underscored the risks associated with unmarked and abandoned RTGs in post-Soviet states.

- **The RTG Theft in Abkhazia (1999):** Another significant RTG-related incident occurred in Abkhazia; a region that had been embroiled in conflict following the dissolution of the Soviet Union. In 1999, thieves stole an RTG from a remote area, likely unaware of the dangers it posed. The RTG was eventually recovered, but not before the radioactive material had caused severe contamination. The theft and subsequent recovery effort highlighted the challenges of securing radioactive materials in conflict zones and the potential for such materials to fall into the wrong hands.

- **The Antarctic RTG Scare (1962):** In the early 1960s, the United States deployed several RTGs in Antarctica to power remote research stations. In 1962, one such RTG was lost in an ice crevasse during a research expedition. The incident sparked concerns about the potential release of radioactive material into the environment. Although the RTG was eventually recovered, the incident prompted a reevaluation of the use of RTGs in environmentally sensitive areas.

- **Russian Lighthouse RTG Abandonment (1990s):** During the 1990s, the Russian Federation faced economic turmoil that led to the abandonment of many RTG-powered lighthouses along its Arctic coast. With the collapse of the Soviet Union, maintenance of these facilities ceased, leaving RTGs exposed to the elements and vulnerable to theft. In several instances, scavengers dismantled RTGs to sell their metal components, exposing themselves to lethal doses of radiation. The abandoned RTGs posed a significant environmental threat, as the radioactive material could potentially leak into the surrounding ecosystem.

Environmental and Health Impacts of RTG Accidents

The environmental and health impacts of RTG accidents can be severe and long-lasting. The radioactive isotopes used in RTGs are highly toxic and can cause serious harm to living organisms if released into the environment. Plutonium-238, for example, emits alpha particles that can cause severe damage to biological tissues if inhaled or ingested. Strontium-90, another commonly used isotope, is known to replace calcium in bones, leading to bone cancer and leukemia.

In cases where RTGs have been damaged or improperly handled, the immediate impact is often acute radiation sickness, characterized by symptoms such as nausea, vomiting, and burns. Long-term exposure to lower levels of radiation can increase the risk of cancer and other health problems.

The environmental contamination resulting from RTG accidents can persist for decades, as radioactive materials slowly decay. Soil and water contamination can affect local ecosystems, and the spread of radioactive particles by wind and water can lead to broader environmental impacts.

The Challenges of RTG Recovery and Disposal

Recovering and safely disposing of damaged or abandoned RTGs is a complex and costly process. In many cases, RTGs are located in remote or hazardous areas, making access difficult. The recovery process often involves extensive planning, specialized equipment, and trained personnel to safely handle and transport the radioactive material.

Once recovered, RTGs must be properly disposed of to prevent further environmental contamination. This typically involves encasing the radioactive material in secure containers and storing it in designated nuclear waste facilities. However, the high cost of recovery and disposal, combined with the logistical challenges, has led to delays and difficulties in addressing abandoned RTGs, particularly in post-Soviet states.

Regulatory and Safety Improvements

In response to the dangers posed by RTGs, regulatory frameworks and safety standards have been developed to minimize the risks associated with their use. International organizations such as the International Atomic Energy Agency (IAEA) have established guidelines for the safe handling, transport, and disposal of RTGs. These guidelines emphasize the importance of proper labeling, secure storage, and regular inspections to prevent accidents.

Countries that use or have used RTGs have also implemented stricter controls to ensure that these devices are not abandoned or improperly handled. Efforts have been made to replace RTGs with safer alternatives, such as solar power or newer, less hazardous nuclear technologies.

Chapter 14: Saint-Laurent Nuclear Power Plant Fire

The Saint-Laurent Nuclear Power Plant, located near the Loire River in the Loir-et-Cher department of France, has been a critical component of the country's energy infrastructure since the late 1960s. Operated by Électricité de France (EDF), the plant initially featured two UNGG (Uranium Naturel Graphite Gaz) reactors, a type of gas-cooled reactor that was a cornerstone of France's early nuclear energy program. Despite its significance in providing electricity to the nation, the plant became the site of two of the most serious nuclear incidents in France's history, particularly the fire in 1980, which remains a stark reminder of the inherent risks associated with nuclear power.

The Background: France's Nuclear Ambitions

In the post-World War II era, France, like many other nations, sought to establish energy independence through the development of nuclear power. The French government invested heavily in nuclear technology, aiming to reduce reliance on foreign oil and establish a self-sufficient energy supply. The UNGG reactor design, developed by the Commissariat à l'Énergie Atomique (CEA), was integral to these early efforts. These reactors were designed to use natural uranium as fuel and graphite as a moderator, with carbon dioxide serving as the coolant.

The Saint-Laurent Nuclear Power Plant was among the first generation of nuclear facilities built in France, with its two UNGG reactors coming online in 1969 and 1971, respectively. The plant was strategically located near the Loire River, which provided a reliable source of water for cooling the reactors. As with many nuclear plants of its era, Saint-Laurent was seen as a symbol of technological progress and national pride.

The Events Leading Up to the Fire

The 1980 fire at the Saint-Laurent Nuclear Power Plant was not the first serious incident at the facility. In fact, just seven years earlier, in 1973, the plant had experienced a partial meltdown in one of its reactors. This earlier incident, which occurred in Reactor A2, involved the melting of fuel elements, but was contained without significant release of radiation. However, it exposed vulnerabilities in the plant's design and operational procedures.

In the years following the 1973 accident, EDF implemented various safety upgrades and operational changes to prevent a recurrence. Despite these efforts, the plant remained a concern for safety regulators and the public, particularly as France's nuclear program expanded and the risks associated with aging reactors became more apparent.

The Fire: March 13, 1980

On March 13, 1980, the Saint-Laurent Nuclear Power Plant became the site of what is widely regarded as France's most severe nuclear incident. The fire occurred in Reactor A1, one of the two UNGG reactors at the facility. The exact sequence of events leading to the fire is complex and involved several technical failures and human errors.

- **Initial Trigger:** The incident began when a cooling system malfunction led to a significant temperature increase in the reactor core. In UNGG reactors, maintaining proper cooling is critical to preventing the graphite moderator from overheating. On this occasion, however, the loss of coolant caused the temperature in the reactor core to rise to dangerous levels.
- **The Fire Outbreak:** As the temperature soared, it eventually caused the graphite moderator to ignite. Graphite, while an effective neutron moderator, can become combustible under

extreme conditions, particularly in the presence of oxygen. The fire that broke out in the reactor core was severe, and flames quickly spread within the reactor building. The fire also damaged the reactor's containment structures, raising concerns about the potential release of radioactive materials.

- **Emergency Response:** The plant's emergency response teams acted quickly to try and bring the situation under control. Firefighting efforts focused on extinguishing the flames within the reactor building and preventing the fire from spreading to other areas of the plant. At the same time, operators worked to cool the reactor core and stabilize the situation. However, these efforts were hampered by several factors. The high radiation levels within the reactor building made it difficult for personnel to approach the fire, and the design of the UNGG reactors, which lacked the robust containment structures found in more modern reactor designs, increased the risk of radioactive release. Additionally, the fire's intensity and the damage it caused to the reactor's systems made it challenging to fully extinguish the flames.

The Aftermath: Containment and Recovery

Despite the challenges, the fire at Saint-Laurent was eventually brought under control, and the reactor core was cooled to prevent further damage. However, the incident left a lasting mark on the plant and the broader French nuclear industry.

- **Radiation Release:** Although the fire did not result in a catastrophic release of radiation, there was a significant release of radioactive particles within the reactor building. Fortunately, the wind conditions at the time and the plant's location limited the dispersion of radioactive material into the environment. Nonetheless, the incident raised serious concerns about the potential for more severe consequences in the event of a similar accident.

- **Cleanup and Decommissioning:** In the immediate aftermath of the fire, extensive cleanup operations were undertaken to remove radioactive contamination from the reactor building and surrounding areas. The damaged reactor, A1, was eventually decommissioned, marking the end of its operational life. The incident also prompted a reevaluation of the safety of the remaining UNGG reactors in France, many of which were subsequently phased out in favor of more modern designs.
- **Public and Political Reactions:** The Saint-Laurent fire had a profound impact on public perception of nuclear energy in France. Although the country had embraced nuclear power as a cornerstone of its energy policy, the incident exposed the risks associated with aging reactors and inadequate safety measures. Public confidence in nuclear power was shaken, leading to increased scrutiny of the nuclear industry and greater demands for transparency and safety improvements. Politically, the incident put pressure on the French government and EDF to demonstrate that they could manage the risks associated with nuclear power. It also influenced the direction of France's nuclear policy, with a greater emphasis on developing safer reactor designs and improving emergency preparedness.

Lessons Learned: Impacts on Nuclear Safety

The Saint-Laurent fire was a pivotal moment in the history of nuclear safety in France. It highlighted several key areas where improvements were needed, both in terms of reactor design and operational procedures.

- **Reactor Design Improvements:** One of the most significant lessons from the Saint-Laurent fire was the need for improved reactor designs that could better withstand extreme conditions and prevent fires or other accidents from escalating. The incident underscored the limitations of the UNGG reactor design, particularly its lack of robust containment structures and its reliance on graphite as a moderator. In response, France accelerated its transition to pressurized water reactors (PWRs), which are more resilient to such incidents. PWRs feature a more advanced containment system and use water, rather than graphite, as a moderator, reducing the risk of fires like the one at Saint-Laurent.

- **Enhanced Emergency Preparedness:** The fire also highlighted the importance of effective emergency preparedness and response. The difficulties faced by the plant's emergency teams in controlling the fire and managing the situation underscored the need for better training, equipment, and protocols. In the years following the incident, EDF and French nuclear regulators implemented significant upgrades to emergency preparedness across the country's nuclear fleet, including regular drills and the development of more sophisticated emergency response plans.

- **Improved Regulatory Oversight:** The Saint-Laurent fire led to greater regulatory oversight of the nuclear industry in France. The French Nuclear Safety Authority (ASN) was given enhanced powers to monitor and enforce safety standards at nuclear facilities. The incident also contributed to the development of more stringent safety regulations, particularly concerning reactor design, operational procedures, and emergency preparedness.

The Broader Impact on Nuclear Policy

The Saint-Laurent fire was not just a technical or operational issue; it had broader implications for France's nuclear policy and its approach to energy security. The incident forced a reevaluation of the risks and benefits of nuclear power, particularly in the context of aging reactors and the potential for severe accidents.

- **Shift Towards Modern Reactor Designs:** In the aftermath of the Saint-Laurent fire, France accelerated its shift away from first-generation reactors like the UNGG and focused on developing and deploying more advanced reactor designs. This shift was part of a broader strategy to ensure the long-term safety and sustainability of the country's nuclear energy program. The development of the PWR, which became the standard reactor design in France, was a key part of this strategy. PWRs are not only safer but also more efficient, making them a more viable option for the future of France's nuclear energy industry.

- **Public and Environmental Concerns:** The incident also heightened public awareness of the environmental and safety risks associated with nuclear power. Environmental groups and anti-nuclear activists used the Saint-Laurent fire as an example of the dangers of nuclear energy, calling for a transition to alternative, renewable energy sources. While nuclear power remained a cornerstone of France's energy policy, the incident contributed to ongoing debates about the role of nuclear energy in the country's energy mix.

- **International Implications:** On an international level, the Saint-Laurent fire was a significant event that drew attention to the risks associated with nuclear power. It served as a cautionary tale for other countries with nuclear programs, particularly those using similar reactor designs. The incident also contributed to global discussions on nuclear safety and the need for international cooperation in managing nuclear risks.

Chapter 15: Zwentendorf Nuclear Power Plant Referendum

In the decades following World War II, many European countries turned to nuclear power as a promising solution to their growing energy needs. The oil crises of the 1970s further underscored the vulnerability of relying on fossil fuels, prompting many nations to invest heavily in nuclear energy. Austria was no exception, and the construction of the Zwentendorf Nuclear Power Plant was part of the country's broader strategy to ensure energy security and reduce dependence on foreign oil. However, the path to nuclear energy in Austria was not without controversy, and the Zwentendorf Nuclear Power Plant referendum of 1978 became a defining moment in the country's energy history.

The Genesis of the Zwentendorf Nuclear Power Plant

The Zwentendorf Nuclear Power Plant, located in the small town of Zwentendorf an der Donau in Lower Austria, was conceived in the 1960s during a period of rapid industrial growth and increasing energy demand in Austria. The Austrian government, eager to modernize the country's energy infrastructure and reduce its reliance on coal and imported oil, saw nuclear power as a viable and forward-looking solution.

In 1969, after years of planning and debate, the Austrian parliament approved the construction of the Zwentendorf Nuclear Power Plant. The plant was designed as a boiling water reactor (BWR), a type of light water nuclear reactor that was widely used in nuclear power stations around the world at the time. The BWR design was considered safe and efficient, with a relatively straightforward construction process. The plant's location on the banks of the Danube River was chosen for its proximity to the capital, Vienna, and the availability of ample cooling water.

Construction of the Zwentendorf plant began in 1972 and proceeded smoothly, with the project moving forward without significant delays. By 1976, the plant was nearly complete, with much of the infrastructure and reactor components already in place. Austria seemed poised to join the ranks of European nations with a robust nuclear power program.

The Rise of the Anti-Nuclear Movement

Despite the progress on the construction of the Zwentendorf plant, opposition to nuclear power was growing both globally and within Austria. The 1970s saw the emergence of a powerful anti-nuclear movement, fueled by growing concerns about the safety of nuclear reactors, the potential for catastrophic accidents, and the long-term environmental and health impacts of nuclear waste.

The anti-nuclear movement in Austria was part of a broader trend across Europe and North America, where environmentalists, scientists, and concerned citizens began to question the wisdom of relying on nuclear power. Several high-profile accidents at nuclear facilities, such as the partial meltdown at the Three Mile Island plant in the United States in 1979, heightened public fears about the potential dangers of nuclear energy.

In Austria, opposition to the Zwentendorf plant coalesced into a formidable political force. Environmental groups, local residents, and some political parties began organizing protests, petitions, and public awareness campaigns to highlight the risks associated with nuclear power. They argued that the plant posed an unacceptable risk to public health and the environment, and that Austria should instead focus on developing alternative, renewable energy sources.

The Political Landscape: Austria's Government and the Nuclear Debate

As opposition to the Zwentendorf plant grew, the political landscape in Austria became increasingly polarized. The ruling Socialist Party of Austria (SPÖ), led by Chancellor Bruno Kreisky, had been a strong supporter of nuclear power and had overseen the approval and construction of the Zwentendorf plant. Kreisky and his government viewed nuclear energy as essential for Austria's economic development and energy independence, particularly in the face of the global energy crisis.

However, as public opposition mounted, the SPÖ found itself under increasing pressure to address the concerns of the anti-nuclear movement. Within the party, there were also divisions, with some members expressing doubts about the safety and desirability of nuclear power. In response to growing public discontent, Kreisky made a surprising political move: he announced that the fate of the Zwentendorf plant would be decided by a national referendum.

The 1978 Referendum: A Nation Decides

On November 5, 1978, Austria held a historic referendum to decide whether the Zwentendorf Nuclear Power Plant should be allowed to start operations. The referendum was a significant event, as it marked the first time in Austrian history that a major infrastructure project would be subject to a direct vote by the people. The decision to hold a referendum was also a testament to the strength of the democratic process in Austria, allowing citizens to have a direct say in the country's energy policy.

The campaign leading up to the referendum was intense and highly polarized. Both proponents and opponents of the plant launched extensive public relations efforts to sway voters. Proponents of the plant, including the SPÖ and many industrial and business leaders, argued that nuclear power was essential for Austria's energy security and economic future. They emphasized the safety measures in place at the Zwentendorf plant and pointed to the success of nuclear power in other countries.

Opponents, on the other hand, focused on the potential dangers of nuclear power, including the risk of accidents, the challenge of managing nuclear waste, and the long-term environmental consequences. They also highlighted alternative energy sources, such as hydroelectric power, which was already well-developed in Austria, as a safer and more sustainable option.

As the referendum date approached, public opinion polls indicated a close race, with a significant portion of the electorate still undecided. The outcome of the vote was uncertain, and both sides mobilized all available resources to influence the final decision.

The Outcome: A Narrow Victory for the Anti-Nuclear Movement

On the day of the referendum, Austrian citizens went to the polls to cast their votes on the future of the Zwentendorf Nuclear Power Plant. The results were close, but in the end, 50.47% of voters opposed the activation of the plant, while 49.53% were in favor. The narrow margin of victory for the anti-nuclear movement was a stunning result, given the significant government and industry support for the plant.

The outcome of the referendum effectively sealed the fate of the Zwentendorf Nuclear Power Plant. Despite being nearly complete and ready for operation, the plant was never activated, and it remains the only nuclear power plant in the world that was fully constructed but never put into service. The referendum result was a clear expression of the Austrian people's will, and it had far-reaching consequences for the country's energy policy.

The Aftermath: Decommissioning and the Legacy of Zwentendorf

Following the referendum, the Austrian government faced the challenge of deciding what to do with the now-unused Zwentendorf Nuclear Power Plant. Although the plant was structurally complete, the decision not to activate it meant that it could not be used for its intended purpose. The government considered several options, including converting the facility to a conventional power plant or using it for research purposes, but none of these options were pursued.

In the end, the Zwentendorf plant was left in a state of preservation, and it remains largely intact to this day. The facility has become a unique symbol of the anti-nuclear movement and a powerful reminder of the potential consequences of public opposition to nuclear energy. The plant is now used for training purposes, as well as for tours and educational programs, offering visitors a glimpse into Austria's nuclear past and the dramatic events that led to the plant's abandonment.

The Zwentendorf referendum also had a profound impact on Austria's broader energy policy. In the years following the vote, Austria shifted its focus away from nuclear power and towards renewable energy sources. The country invested heavily in hydroelectric power, wind energy, and later, solar energy, making significant strides in reducing its reliance on fossil fuels and establishing itself as a leader in renewable energy.

Austria's Anti-Nuclear Stance: From Zwentendorf to the Present

The Zwentendorf referendum marked a turning point in Austria's relationship with nuclear energy. The decision to abandon the plant reflected a broader rejection of nuclear power in Austrian society, and it set the stage for the country's ongoing anti-nuclear stance.

In 1999, Austria passed a law that formally banned the use of nuclear power for electricity generation. The law, known as the Nuclear-Free

Austria Act, reinforced the country's commitment to a nuclear-free energy policy and prohibited the construction of new nuclear power plants on Austrian soil. This law remains in force today and is a cornerstone of Austria's energy policy.

Austria's anti-nuclear stance has also extended beyond its borders. The country has been an active participant in international efforts to promote nuclear disarmament and non-proliferation, and it has frequently voiced opposition to the expansion of nuclear power in neighboring countries. Austria's strong anti-nuclear position has made it a vocal advocate for alternative energy sources and has contributed to its reputation as a leader in environmental protection and sustainable development.

The Broader Impact: Lessons from Zwentendorf

The Zwentendorf Nuclear Power Plant referendum is more than just a historical event in Austria's energy history; it is a case study in the power of public opinion and the democratic process in shaping energy policy. The referendum demonstrated that when citizens are given a direct voice in decisions that affect their lives and their environment, they can have a profound impact on the direction of national policy.

The Zwentendorf case also offers important lessons for other countries grappling with the challenges of energy policy and public engagement. It highlights the importance of transparency, public involvement, and the need for governments to listen to the concerns of their citizens. In an era where environmental and energy issues are increasingly at the forefront of public discourse, the Zwentendorf referendum serves as a reminder that the decisions we make today will have lasting consequences for future generations.

Chapter 16: Dounreay Fast Reactor Incidents

The Dounreay Nuclear Establishment, located on the northern coast of Scotland near Thurso, was once the crown jewel of the United Kingdom's ambitious nuclear energy program. Established in the 1950s as a center for research and development into fast breeder reactor technology, Dounreay played a pivotal role in the UK's efforts to harness the power of nuclear energy for both civilian and military purposes. Among its most notable projects was the Dounreay Fast Reactor (DFR), a prototype fast breeder reactor designed to produce more fuel than it consumed, a concept that promised an almost limitless supply of energy.

However, the history of Dounreay is also marked by a series of incidents and accidents that have cast a long shadow over the site and raised serious concerns about the safety of fast reactor technology. The Dounreay Fast Reactor incidents, which occurred during the 1960s and 1970s, were among the most significant nuclear events in the UK, highlighting the risks and challenges associated with the operation of fast reactors. This detailed analysis explores the history of the DFR, the incidents that occurred, their causes and consequences, and the long-term impact on nuclear policy in the UK.

The Dounreay Fast Reactor: Ambitions and Design

The Dounreay Fast Reactor, also known as DFR, was conceived as part of the UK's broader strategy to develop advanced nuclear technologies that could provide a sustainable and secure energy supply. The concept of a fast breeder reactor was particularly appealing because it offered the potential to generate more fissile material than it consumed, effectively creating a "breeder" cycle that could extend the supply of nuclear fuel far beyond the limits of conventional reactors.

- **Design and Construction:** The DFR was a sodium-cooled fast reactor, meaning it used liquid sodium as a coolant instead of water, which is used in most conventional reactors. Sodium has excellent thermal properties, allowing for more efficient heat transfer and higher operating temperatures. These characteristics made sodium an ideal choice for fast reactors, which operate at much higher temperatures and neutron energies than thermal reactors. The core of the DFR was designed to contain a mixture of uranium and plutonium fuel, with a surrounding blanket of fertile material, typically uranium-238. As the reactor operated, fast neutrons from the fission process would convert the fertile material into new fissile fuel, effectively "breeding" more fuel than was initially loaded into the reactor. This process promised to create a self-sustaining cycle that could significantly reduce the need for fresh uranium and extend the life of nuclear fuel resources.

- **Construction Timeline and Early Operations:** Construction of the DFR began in the mid-1950s, with the reactor becoming operational in 1959. At the time, it was one of the most advanced nuclear reactors in the world and represented a significant technological achievement for the UK. The reactor had a thermal output of 60 megawatts, making it relatively small compared to modern nuclear reactors, but it was primarily intended as a prototype and research reactor rather than a full-scale power plant. The early years of the DFR's operation were marked by a sense of optimism and confidence in the potential of fast breeder technology. The reactor operated successfully for several years, and the knowledge gained from its operation contributed to the development of subsequent fast reactor designs in the UK and abroad. However, this period of optimism would soon be overshadowed by a series of incidents that exposed the challenges and dangers associated with fast reactors.

The Sodium Leak Incident of 1965

One of the first major incidents at the Dounreay Fast Reactor occurred in 1965, when a leak of liquid sodium coolant was discovered. Sodium is highly reactive, particularly when it comes into contact with water or air, and a leak in the reactor's coolant system posed a serious risk of fire or explosion.

- **The Incident:** The leak was detected during routine inspections of the reactor's cooling system. A small crack had developed in one of the coolant pipes, allowing liquid sodium to escape. Fortunately, the leak was detected early, and the reactor was quickly shut down to prevent the situation from escalating. Emergency teams were able to isolate the affected section of the cooling system and contain the leak before any significant damage occurred.

- **Response and Consequences:** The incident was a wake-up call for the operators of the DFR and the broader nuclear industry. While no radioactive material was released, and there were no injuries, the incident highlighted the inherent risks associated with using sodium as a coolant. The reactivity of sodium, combined with the high temperatures and pressures inside a fast reactor, meant that even a small leak could have potentially catastrophic consequences. In response to the incident, the reactor was taken offline for several months while repairs were carried out and additional safety measures were implemented. The incident also led to a reassessment of the design and operation of fast reactors, with a particular focus on the integrity of the coolant system and the need for more robust leak detection and containment measures.

The Explosion in 1977: The Breeder Fuel Incident

The most significant and widely publicized incident at the Dounreay Fast Reactor occurred in 1977, when an explosion rocked the reactor complex. This event, often referred to as the "breeder fuel incident," was a major setback for the UK's fast reactor program and raised serious questions about the future of fast breeder technology.

- **The Incident:** The explosion occurred in a storage facility adjacent to the DFR, where breeder fuel elements were being prepared for reprocessing. These fuel elements, which had been used in the reactor's core and blanket, contained a mixture of uranium, plutonium, and fission products, making them highly radioactive and chemically reactive. On May 10, 1977, a chemical reaction occurred in one of the fuel storage containers, leading to a buildup of gas pressure. The exact cause of the reaction is still debated, but it is believed that moisture had entered the container, possibly during handling or storage. When the gas pressure reached a critical level, the container exploded, releasing radioactive material and debris into the storage facility.
- **Immediate Response and Containment Efforts:** The explosion caused significant damage to the storage facility, but fortunately, it did not result in a major release of radioactive material into the environment. The design of the facility, with its thick concrete walls and reinforced structures, helped contain the explosion and prevent a more widespread contamination. However, the incident was still serious enough to prompt a full-scale emergency response. The affected area was immediately sealed off, and workers were evacuated from the site. Radiation levels were monitored closely, and decontamination efforts were initiated to remove radioactive debris and prevent any further spread of contamination.

- **Investigation and Root Cause Analysis:** An investigation into the incident was launched by the United Kingdom Atomic Energy Authority (UKAEA), which operated the Dounreay site. The investigation focused on determining the cause of the explosion and identifying any failures in the handling and storage procedures for breeder fuel. The inquiry revealed several contributing factors, including the possible ingress of moisture into the storage container, inadequate monitoring of gas pressures, and weaknesses in the procedures for handling and storing highly reactive materials. The investigation also highlighted the challenges of managing the complex chemical and radiological properties of breeder fuel, which required specialized knowledge and equipment. As a result of the investigation, several changes were made to the handling and storage procedures for breeder fuel at Dounreay and other nuclear facilities. These included improved monitoring of gas pressures, enhanced training for personnel, and stricter controls on the storage conditions for radioactive materials.

Long-Term Impact: The Decline of Fast Breeder Technology in the UK

The incidents at the Dounreay Fast Reactor had a profound impact on the UK's nuclear program and contributed to a growing sense of caution regarding the future of fast breeder technology. While the DFR continued to operate for a few more years after the 1977 explosion, the momentum behind the fast breeder program began to wane.

- **Shift in Government Policy:** By the late 1970s, the UK government and the nuclear industry were beginning to reassess the viability of fast breeder reactors as a cornerstone of the country's energy policy. The high costs, technical challenges, and safety risks associated with fast reactors, as evidenced by the incidents at Dounreay, made them less attractive compared to other nuclear technologies, such as light water reactors, which were already widely deployed. In the early 1980s, the UK government decided to scale back its investment in fast breeder technology, effectively marking the end of the Dounreay Fast Reactor program. The DFR was finally shut down in 1977, and decommissioning efforts began shortly thereafter. The decision to abandon the fast breeder program was influenced not only by the incidents at Dounreay but also by changing energy priorities and the availability of alternative energy sources.

- **Decommissioning and Cleanup:** The decommissioning of the DFR and the broader Dounreay site has been a long and complex process, reflecting the challenges of dismantling a nuclear facility that was at the forefront of experimental reactor technology. Decommissioning work has involved the removal of radioactive materials, the dismantling of reactor components, and the cleanup of contaminated areas. One of the most significant challenges has been dealing with the sodium coolant, which must be carefully managed to prevent chemical reactions and ensure safe disposal. The UKAEA and its successor organizations have developed specialized techniques for handling and disposing of sodium, as well as for managing the radioactive waste generated by the reactor. Decommissioning of the Dounreay site is still ongoing, with the goal of eventually returning the site to a state where it can be used for other purposes. The process has been marked by significant technical and logistical challenges, but it has also provided valuable lessons for the decommissioning of other nuclear facilities around the world.

Lessons Learned: Safety and the Future of Nuclear Energy

The incidents at the Dounreay Fast Reactor, particularly the sodium leak in 1965 and the breeder fuel explosion in 1977, offer important lessons for the nuclear industry and for the broader debate over the future of nuclear energy.

- **Safety Culture and Risk Management:** One of the key lessons from the Dounreay incidents is the importance of a strong safety culture and effective risk management in the operation of nuclear facilities. The challenges of working with fast reactors, which involve highly reactive materials and complex physical and chemical processes, require a rigorous approach to safety that anticipates and mitigates potential risks. The incidents at Dounreay also underscore the need for continuous monitoring and maintenance of nuclear facilities, particularly when dealing with advanced reactor technologies that may not be as well understood as conventional reactors. The early detection of the sodium leak in 1965, for example, helped prevent a potentially catastrophic accident, highlighting the value of proactive safety measures.

- **Public Perception and Trust:** The Dounreay incidents also had a significant impact on public perception of nuclear energy in the UK. The explosion in 1977, in particular, was widely reported in the media and contributed to growing concerns about the safety of nuclear power. Public trust in the nuclear industry was eroded by these incidents, and this loss of trust has had long-term implications for the acceptance of nuclear energy as a viable and safe energy source. Building and maintaining public trust is a critical challenge for the nuclear industry, particularly in the aftermath of incidents that raise questions about safety and transparency. The Dounreay experience demonstrates the importance of clear communication, accountability, and transparency in addressing public concerns and ensuring that the risks associated with nuclear energy are properly managed.

- **The Future of Fast Reactor Technology:** While the Dounreay Fast Reactor was ultimately shut down, and the UK's fast breeder program was largely abandoned, the concept of fast reactor technology has not disappeared. In recent years, there has been renewed interest in fast reactors as part of a broader effort to develop advanced nuclear technologies that can address the challenges of climate change and energy security. Fast reactors, including new designs such as the Generation IV reactors, offer the potential for more efficient use of nuclear fuel, reduced nuclear waste, and enhanced safety features. However, the lessons learned from the Dounreay incidents remain highly relevant, particularly in terms of the need for rigorous safety standards, effective risk management, and a strong safety culture. As the global nuclear industry continues to explore advanced reactor technologies, the experience of Dounreay serves as a reminder of the challenges and risks involved in developing and operating fast reactors. The lessons of Dounreay should inform the design, construction, and operation of future fast reactors, ensuring that safety is always the top priority.

Chapter 17: Savannah River Site Incidents

The Savannah River Site (SRS), located in South Carolina near the Savannah River, has been a central component of the United States' nuclear program since its establishment in the early 1950s. Initially constructed as a nuclear weapons production facility, SRS played a crucial role in the Cold War, producing plutonium and tritium for the nation's nuclear arsenal. Over the decades, the site has evolved to include nuclear research, waste management, and environmental cleanup operations, becoming one of the most complex and heavily regulated nuclear sites in the world.

However, the history of the Savannah River Site is also marked by a series of incidents and accidents that have raised significant concerns about the safety and environmental impact of nuclear operations. These incidents, which span from the early years of the site's operation to more recent times, have had far-reaching consequences for the workers at the site, the surrounding communities, and the broader debate over the safety of nuclear energy and weapons production.

This detailed analysis examines the key incidents at the Savannah River Site, exploring their causes, consequences, and the lessons learned. The narrative of SRS is a powerful reminder of the challenges and responsibilities associated with nuclear technology, as well as the ongoing efforts to manage the legacy of the nuclear age.

The Establishment of the Savannah River Site: Cold War Imperatives

- **Origins and Strategic Importance:** The Savannah River Site was established in 1950 by the U.S. Atomic Energy Commission (AEC) as part of the nation's strategic response to the growing threat of the Soviet Union during the Cold War. The decision to build the site was driven by the need to produce weapons-grade plutonium and tritium, essential components for the hydrogen bomb, which was then under development. The location in South Carolina was chosen for its relative remoteness, access to large volumes of water from the Savannah River for cooling purposes, and proximity to existing infrastructure.

- **Construction and Early Operations:** Construction of the Savannah River Site began in 1951, and the site quickly became one of the largest and most complex industrial facilities in the United States. At its peak, SRS employed tens of thousands of workers and operated five nuclear reactors, a chemical separation plant, and numerous support facilities. The reactors were used to irradiate uranium and produce plutonium and tritium, while the chemical separation plant processed the irradiated fuel to extract these materials. From its inception, the Savannah River Site was shrouded in secrecy, with much of its operations classified to protect national security. This secrecy, combined with the scale and complexity of the site, contributed to a culture that prioritized production goals over safety and environmental considerations. This culture would later be implicated in several incidents that highlighted the risks associated with large-scale nuclear production.

Early Incidents: Reactor Malfunctions and Safety Concerns

The first significant incidents at the Savannah River Site occurred during the 1950s and 1960s, as the site's reactors were brought online and began full-scale production. These early incidents, while not as severe as later events, foreshadowed the challenges that would come to define the site's history.

- **Reactor Malfunctions:** The reactors at SRS were among the most advanced in the world at the time, but they were also complex and prone to malfunctions. One of the earliest incidents occurred in 1956, when a cooling system failure in one of the reactors led to an unplanned shutdown. While the situation was quickly brought under control, it raised concerns about the reliability of the reactor systems and the adequacy of safety protocols. Another significant incident occurred in 1960, when a partial meltdown of a fuel assembly was detected in one of the reactors. This incident, though contained, highlighted the potential dangers of reactor operation and the need for improved monitoring and safety systems. The response to these early incidents included upgrades to reactor control systems, enhanced training for operators, and a greater emphasis on safety procedures.

- **Worker Safety and Radiation Exposure:** Worker safety was a growing concern during the early years of the Savannah River Site's operation. The nature of the work—handling highly radioactive materials and operating large-scale nuclear reactors—posed significant risks to the health and safety of the workforce. Radiation exposure was a particular concern, with many workers exposed to higher-than-acceptable levels of radiation due to inadequate shielding, poor ventilation, and insufficient protective equipment. In 1957, an incident occurred in which several workers were exposed to high levels of radiation during a maintenance operation on one of the reactors. The workers were not adequately informed of the risks, and the incident led to a reevaluation of safety practices at the site. As a result, new protocols were introduced to reduce radiation exposure, including stricter controls on access to high-radiation areas, improved protective gear, and more rigorous training for workers.

The 1970s: Tritium Releases and Environmental Concerns

The 1970s were a period of increasing environmental awareness in the United States, and the Savannah River Site was not immune to the growing scrutiny of industrial pollution and its impacts on the environment. During this decade, several incidents occurred that raised serious concerns about the environmental impact of operations at SRS, particularly with regard to the release of radioactive materials into the surrounding environment.

- **Tritium Releases into the Savannah River:** Tritium, a radioactive isotope of hydrogen, was one of the primary products of the reactors at SRS, and its production was essential for maintaining the U.S. nuclear arsenal. However, tritium is also highly mobile in the environment, readily mixing with water and spreading through groundwater and surface water systems. During the 1970s, it was discovered that significant amounts of tritium were being released from the Savannah River Site into the Savannah River, which serves as a vital water source for communities downstream. These releases were the result of routine discharges from the reactors and processing facilities, as well as leaks from storage tanks and waste disposal sites.
- **Environmental and Public Health Impacts:** The discovery of tritium contamination in the Savannah River raised alarm among environmentalists, public health officials, and the general public. Tritium, while not as dangerous as some other radioactive materials, still poses a risk to human health, particularly when ingested through contaminated water. Prolonged exposure to tritium can increase the risk of cancer and other health problems. The releases of tritium also highlighted broader concerns about the environmental management practices at SRS. The site had been designed

primarily with production goals in mind, and environmental protection was often a secondary consideration. The discovery of tritium contamination prompted calls for greater oversight and regulation of the site's operations, as well as for more comprehensive environmental monitoring and remediation efforts.

- **Regulatory Response and Cleanup Efforts:** In response to the tritium releases, the U.S. Environmental Protection Agency (EPA) and other regulatory agencies began to take a more active role in overseeing the environmental management practices at the Savannah River Site. This included stricter limits on radioactive discharges, enhanced monitoring of water and soil for contamination, and the development of plans for cleaning up contaminated areas. One of the most significant challenges in addressing tritium contamination was the long half-life of tritium, which means that it can remain in the environment for extended periods. Cleanup efforts at SRS have included the installation of groundwater treatment systems, the containment of contaminated soil, and the monitoring of tritium levels in the river and surrounding areas. These efforts have helped to reduce the levels of tritium in the environment, but the legacy of contamination continues to be a concern.

The 1980s: The Cold War's End and the Beginning of Decommissioning

The 1980s marked a turning point for the Savannah River Site, as the Cold War began to wind down and the demand for nuclear weapons production decreased. This period saw a shift in focus from production to cleanup and decommissioning, as well as the beginning of efforts to address the environmental and safety challenges that had accumulated over the previous decades.

- **Reduction in Nuclear Production:** As the Cold War drew to a close, the need for new nuclear weapons declined, and the U.S. government began to scale back its nuclear production facilities. At the Savannah River Site, this shift was most evident in the reduction of tritium production, as well as the eventual shutdown of several of the site's reactors. The reduction in nuclear production was accompanied by a growing recognition of the need to address the environmental and health impacts of past operations. This included the remediation of contaminated sites, the safe disposal of nuclear waste, and the decommissioning of aging facilities. The transition from production to cleanup presented significant challenges, both in terms of technical complexity and the need for ongoing funding and regulatory oversight.

- **Safety Incidents and Worker Exposure:** Despite the reduction in production activities, the 1980s were not without safety incidents at the Savannah River Site. One notable incident occurred in 1984, when a fire broke out in one of the site's plutonium processing facilities. The fire, which was caused by a chemical reaction involving highly reactive materials, resulted in the release of radioactive particles within the facility. While the fire was quickly contained, several workers were exposed to elevated levels of radiation, and the incident raised concerns about the safety of aging infrastructure and equipment at the site. In addition to the fire, there were also reports of ongoing issues with worker safety, including exposure to hazardous chemicals and radiation. These incidents highlighted the challenges of maintaining safety standards in a facility that was increasingly focused on decommissioning and cleanup rather than production. The incidents also underscored the need for continued investment in safety training, equipment upgrades, and regulatory oversight to protect workers and the surrounding communities.

The 1990s: Environmental Cleanup and Legacy Waste Management

The 1990s were a period of intensive environmental cleanup and waste management at the Savannah River Site, as the U.S. Department of Energy (DOE) and its contractors worked to address the legacy of contamination and waste generated by decades of nuclear production. This period also saw a growing emphasis on public involvement and transparency in the management of the site, as well as ongoing challenges in dealing with the complex and hazardous materials that remained.

- **High-Level Waste Tanks:** One of the most pressing challenges at the Savannah River Site during the 1990s was the management of high-level radioactive waste stored in underground tanks. These tanks, which had been used to store liquid waste from the processing of nuclear materials, contained a mixture of highly radioactive sludge, salt, and liquid waste. Over time, concerns grew about the integrity of the tanks, many of which were approaching or exceeding their intended design life. In 1993, a leak was discovered in one of the high-level waste tanks, prompting an urgent response from the DOE and its contractors. The leak raised fears of groundwater contamination and highlighted the risks associated with the long-term storage of radioactive waste. In response, the DOE accelerated efforts to develop and implement a plan for stabilizing and ultimately closing the high-level waste tanks.
- **The Defense Waste Processing Facility:** A key component of the cleanup effort was the construction and operation of

the Defense Waste Processing Facility (DWPF), which began operating in 1996. The DWPF was designed to vitrify (solidify) high-level radioactive waste by mixing it with glass-forming materials and heating it to create a stable glass form. This process significantly reduced the volume of waste and made it safer for long-term storage and eventual disposal. The operation of the DWPF represented a major milestone in the cleanup of the Savannah River Site, as it provided a means of safely processing and immobilizing the most hazardous waste at the site. However, the complexity of the vitrification process and the challenges of dealing with a wide range of waste types meant that the cleanup effort would be a long-term endeavor, with ongoing technical and regulatory challenges.

- **Public Involvement and Environmental Justice:** During the 1990s, there was also a growing emphasis on public involvement and environmental justice in the management of the Savannah River Site. Communities living near the site, many of which were historically disadvantaged and disproportionately affected by environmental pollution, increasingly demanded a greater voice in decisions affecting their health and environment. The DOE responded by establishing advisory boards and engaging in more transparent communication with the public. These efforts were aimed at rebuilding trust and ensuring that the concerns of local communities were addressed in the cleanup and decommissioning process. However, tensions remained, particularly over issues such as the pace of cleanup, the potential for future contamination, and the long-term management of nuclear waste.

The 21st Century: Ongoing Challenges and the Future of the Savannah River Site

As the Savannah River Site entered the 21st century, it continued to face significant challenges related to the legacy of nuclear production and the ongoing need for environmental cleanup and waste management. The site's role in the U.S. nuclear program also evolved, with a greater focus on research, non-proliferation, and the safe management of nuclear materials.

- **Ongoing Waste Management and Cleanup:** The management of radioactive waste remains a central challenge at the Savannah River Site. While significant progress has been made in stabilizing and processing high-level waste, large volumes of waste still require long-term storage and monitoring. The closure of the high-level waste tanks and the continued operation of the DWPF are critical components of the site's ongoing cleanup efforts, but the complexity of the waste and the risks associated with long-term storage mean that this work will continue for decades to come. In addition to high-level waste, the site also contains a range of other radioactive and hazardous materials, including contaminated soil, groundwater, and infrastructure. The cleanup of these materials requires a combination of advanced technologies, regulatory oversight, and ongoing monitoring to ensure that the environment and public health are protected.
- **New Missions and Research:** In recent years, the Savannah River Site has taken on new missions related to nuclear research, non-proliferation, and the management of surplus nuclear materials. The site is home to several research facilities, including the Savannah River National Laboratory, which conducts research on nuclear materials, environmental science, and energy technologies. The site's role in non-

proliferation efforts includes the processing and storage of surplus weapons-grade plutonium, as well as the conversion of highly enriched uranium to low-enriched uranium for use in nuclear reactors. These activities are part of broader efforts to reduce the global stockpile of nuclear weapons materials and promote the peaceful use of nuclear energy.

- **Community and Economic Impact:** The Savannah River Site remains a major economic engine for the surrounding region, providing jobs and economic opportunities for thousands of workers. However, the transition from production to cleanup and research has also brought challenges, including the need to diversify the local economy and ensure that the workforce has the skills needed for new and emerging roles at the site. The site's future will also depend on continued investment in cleanup and research activities, as well as the ability to address the long-term challenges of managing nuclear materials and waste. The legacy of the Savannah River Site is a complex one, marked by both the successes and failures of the nuclear age, and the ongoing efforts to manage its impact will shape the region for generations to come.

Chapter 18: Lucens Reactor Accident

The Lucens Reactor accident, Switzerland's most significant nuclear incident, is a largely forgotten chapter in the history of nuclear power. Occurring on January 21, 1969, the accident was a critical moment in the development of nuclear energy in Switzerland and had profound implications for the country's energy policies and safety standards.

In the 1950s and 1960s, many countries, including Switzerland, were exploring nuclear power as a potential solution to energy needs and as a way to demonstrate technological prowess. Switzerland, a neutral country with limited natural resources, was particularly interested in developing nuclear technology as a means of ensuring energy independence. The Lucens reactor, a small, experimental power reactor, was a key part of this strategy.

However, the accident at the Lucens reactor not only halted Switzerland's progress in nuclear technology but also served as a stark reminder of the risks associated with nuclear energy. In this detailed analysis, we will explore the background of the Lucens reactor, the events leading up to the accident, the accident itself, and its aftermath. We will also examine the lessons learned from the incident and its long-term impact on Switzerland's nuclear policy.

The Lucens Reactor: Background and Design

- **Origins of the Lucens Project:** The Lucens reactor project was initiated in the mid-1950s as part of Switzerland's efforts to develop its own nuclear power capabilities. The reactor was designed as an experimental heavy water reactor, using natural uranium as fuel and heavy water as a moderator. This design was chosen for its potential to operate without the need for enriched uranium, which was expensive and difficult to obtain. The Swiss government saw the Lucens project as a way to demonstrate the country's ability to develop advanced nuclear technology. The project was overseen by the Federal Institute for Reactor Research (EIR), and construction of the reactor began in 1962 in an underground cavern near the town of Lucens in the Canton of Vaud. The underground location was chosen for safety reasons, as it provided natural protection against radiation and containment of any potential accidents.

- **Reactor Design and Technical Specifications:** The Lucens reactor was a small, pilot-scale reactor with a thermal power output of 30 megawatts (MW). It was a heavy water-moderated, gas-cooled reactor, similar in concept to the CANDU reactors developed in Canada. The reactor core consisted of natural uranium fuel rods arranged in a lattice structure and surrounded by heavy water, which acted as both a moderator and a coolant. The heavy water was contained in a calandria, a large cylindrical vessel that housed the reactor core. The reactor was also equipped with a sophisticated system of control rods, which were used to regulate the nuclear reaction by absorbing neutrons and controlling the rate of fission. The gas coolant, carbon dioxide (CO_2), was circulated through the reactor core to remove heat, which was then transferred to a secondary water loop to produce steam and generate electricity. The reactor design was innovative and complex, reflecting Switzerland's ambition to develop a unique approach to nuclear power. However, the complexity of the design also introduced significant technical challenges, particularly in the areas of reactor control, cooling, and safety.

Construction and Early Operation: Technical Challenges and Setbacks

- **Construction Difficulties:** The construction of the Lucens reactor was marked by a number of technical challenges and delays. The underground location, while providing safety advantages, also presented significant engineering difficulties, particularly in terms of ventilation, access, and the installation of equipment. Additionally, the use of natural uranium and heavy water as a moderator required careful handling and precise control of the reactor's operation. During construction, there were also concerns about the reactor's cooling system, particularly the use of CO_2 as a coolant. CO_2, while effective as a gas coolant, has a lower heat capacity than water, which meant that the cooling system had to be carefully designed and operated to ensure that the reactor remained within safe temperature limits.

- **Initial Operation and Testing:** The Lucens reactor achieved its first criticality (the point at which a nuclear chain reaction becomes self-sustaining) in 1966, and initial testing and operation began shortly thereafter. The early tests were generally successful, and the reactor operated at low power for extended periods to evaluate its performance and gather data on its behavior. However, even during these early tests, there were signs of potential problems. The reactor's control system, which relied on a combination of mechanical and electronic components, was found to be less reliable than anticipated, leading to concerns about the ability to safely control the reactor under all conditions. Additionally, the CO_2 cooling system showed signs of instability, with fluctuations in pressure and temperature that were difficult to manage. Despite these challenges, the Lucens reactor was seen as a promising demonstration of Swiss nuclear technology, and plans were made to gradually increase its power output and begin producing electricity for the grid.

The 1969 Accident: Sequence of Events and Root Causes

- **The Lead-Up to the Accident:** In late 1968, the Lucens reactor was undergoing a routine maintenance shutdown, during which the reactor was partially disassembled, and the fuel rods were removed for inspection. This maintenance period was intended to ensure that the reactor was operating safely and that there were no signs of damage or wear in the reactor core or other critical components. However, during this shutdown, a key error was made: a CO_2 leak occurred in the reactor's cooling system, allowing moisture to enter the reactor core. This moisture reacted with the magnesium alloy cladding of the fuel rods, causing them to corrode. The corrosion weakened the cladding, creating a significant risk of a rupture when the reactor was restarted.

- **The Day of the Accident:** On January 21, 1969, the Lucens reactor was restarted following the maintenance shutdown. Almost immediately, the operators noticed abnormal readings from the reactor's instrumentation, including elevated temperatures and pressure in the reactor core. These readings indicated that something was seriously wrong, and the decision was made to shut down the reactor. Unfortunately, the shutdown process was not fast enough to prevent a catastrophic failure. The corrosion in the fuel rods, exacerbated by the presence of moisture and the heat generated during the restart, led to a rupture in one or more of the fuel elements. This rupture released radioactive material into the reactor core, and the resulting reaction caused a partial meltdown of the reactor. The pressure inside the reactor vessel increased rapidly, leading to the release of CO_2 gas and radioactive particles into the underground cavern. The containment system, while effective in preventing the release of radiation into the environment, was not able to fully contain the internal contamination, and the reactor building itself became highly radioactive.

- **Immediate Response and Containment:** The immediate response to the accident was focused on ensuring the safety of the reactor operators and preventing any further release of radiation. The control room, which was located outside the underground cavern, was quickly evacuated, and a team of specialists was assembled to assess the situation and develop a plan for containing the incident. Fortunately, the design of the Lucens reactor, with its underground location and robust containment structures, helped to prevent a more serious release of radiation. The radioactive materials were largely confined to the reactor building, and there was no significant release into the environment. However, the reactor core was severely damaged, and the facility was heavily contaminated with radioactive materials.

The Aftermath: Cleanup, Investigation, and Long-Term Impact

- **Cleanup and Decommissioning:** The cleanup of the Lucens reactor site was a complex and challenging process that took several years to complete. The first priority was to stabilize the reactor and prevent any further release of radioactive material. This involved sealing off the reactor core and surrounding areas, as well as installing additional ventilation and filtration systems to reduce the risk of airborne contamination. Once the reactor was stabilized, the focus shifted to the decommissioning of the facility and the safe disposal of the radioactive waste. The damaged reactor core and other contaminated materials were carefully removed from the site and transported to specialized facilities for long-term storage. The underground cavern was then decontaminated, and the reactor building was sealed and monitored for any signs of residual radiation. The decommissioning process was completed in the early 1970s, and the Lucens reactor site was eventually returned to a natural state. However, the accident had a lasting impact on the Swiss nuclear program, leading to a reevaluation of the country's approach to nuclear energy and a renewed emphasis on safety and regulation.

- **Investigation and Analysis:** The investigation into the Lucens reactor accident was conducted by a team of experts from the Federal Institute for Reactor Research (EIR) and other Swiss government agencies. The investigation focused on determining the root causes of the accident, as well as identifying any design or operational failures that may have contributed to the incident. The investigation revealed that the primary cause of the accident was the corrosion of the fuel rod cladding, which was caused by the ingress of moisture during the maintenance shutdown. The moisture, which had entered the reactor core due to a CO_2 leak, reacted with the magnesium alloy cladding, weakening it and making it susceptible to rupture when the reactor was restarted. The investigation also identified several secondary factors that contributed to the accident, including deficiencies in the reactor's control system, inadequate maintenance procedures, and a lack of proper oversight and regulation. These findings led to a series of recommendations for improving the safety of nuclear reactors in Switzerland, including the need for more rigorous maintenance protocols, better training for reactor operators, and enhanced regulatory oversight.
- **Impact on Swiss Nuclear Policy:** The Lucens reactor accident had a profound impact on Switzerland's nuclear policy and its approach to nuclear energy. In the wake of the accident, the Swiss government decided to abandon plans for

further development of heavy water reactors and instead focused on more conventional light water reactors, which were considered to be safer and more reliable. The accident also led to the establishment of a more robust regulatory framework for nuclear energy in Switzerland. The Federal Nuclear Safety Inspectorate (ENSI) was given greater authority to oversee the operation of nuclear facilities, and new safety standards were introduced to ensure that similar accidents could be prevented in the future. Public perception of nuclear energy in Switzerland was also affected by the Lucens accident. While the incident did not lead to widespread opposition to nuclear power, it did raise awareness of the risks associated with nuclear technology and contributed to a more cautious and measured approach to its development.

Lessons Learned: The Legacy of the Lucens Reactor Accident

- **Importance of Safety Culture:** One of the key lessons from the Lucens reactor accident is the importance of a strong safety culture in the operation of nuclear facilities. The accident demonstrated that even small errors or oversights in maintenance and operation can have serious consequences, particularly in the context of complex and potentially hazardous technologies like nuclear reactors. The Lucens incident highlighted the need for rigorous safety protocols, regular training and retraining of personnel, and a culture of continuous improvement and vigilance. These principles have since become central to the operation of nuclear facilities around the world and are considered essential for ensuring the safe and reliable use of nuclear energy.

- **Design and Operational Challenges:** The Lucens reactor accident also underscored the challenges associated with innovative or experimental reactor designs. While the heavy water, gas-cooled design of the Lucens reactor offered certain advantages, it also introduced significant technical complexities that ultimately contributed to the accident. The incident highlighted the importance of thorough testing and validation of new reactor designs before they are put into operation, as well as the need for careful consideration of potential failure modes and the implementation of robust safety systems to mitigate risks.

- **Regulatory Oversight and Public Confidence:** Finally, the Lucens reactor accident emphasized the critical role of regulatory oversight in the safe operation of nuclear facilities. The accident revealed gaps in the oversight and regulation of the Lucens project, which allowed certain safety issues to go unaddressed until it was too late. In response to the accident, Switzerland strengthened its regulatory framework for nuclear energy, ensuring that future projects would be subject to more rigorous scrutiny and oversight. This has helped to maintain public confidence in the safety of nuclear energy in Switzerland and has contributed to the country's continued use of nuclear power as part of its energy mix.

Chapter 19: Marcoule Nuclear Site Accident

The Marcoule Nuclear Site, located in southern France near the Rhône River, is one of the country's oldest and most significant nuclear facilities. Established in 1955, Marcoule has been a cornerstone of France's nuclear energy and defense programs. The site has been involved in various activities, including the production of plutonium for nuclear weapons, the reprocessing of nuclear fuel, and the development of advanced nuclear reactors. It has also been home to a number of experimental reactors and facilities dedicated to research and development in nuclear technology.

Given its central role in France's nuclear history, the Marcoule site has also been the location of several notable incidents. Among these, the most significant is the accident that occurred on September 12, 2011, at the Centraco (Centre de Traitement et de Conditionnement des Déchets Faiblement Radioactifs) facility. This accident, while not on the scale of disasters like Chernobyl or Fukushima, nonetheless raised serious concerns about nuclear safety, especially in the context of waste management and processing.

In this detailed exploration, we will delve into the background of the Marcoule Nuclear Site, the events leading up to the 2011 accident, the accident itself, and its aftermath. We will also discuss the broader implications for nuclear safety and waste management, particularly in France, and the lessons learned from this incident.

The Marcoule Nuclear Site: Background and Historical Context

- **Origins and Early Development:** The Marcoule Nuclear Site was established in 1955 as part of France's post-war efforts to develop nuclear energy and technology. The site's primary purpose was to produce plutonium for France's burgeoning nuclear weapons program. The early reactors at Marcoule, including the G1, G2, and G3 reactors, were gas-cooled, graphite-moderated reactors specifically designed for plutonium production. These reactors were among the first of their kind in France and represented a significant step forward in the country's nuclear capabilities. As France's nuclear energy program expanded in the 1960s and 1970s, Marcoule's role also evolved. In addition to its military functions, the site became a hub for research and development in civilian nuclear technology. Marcoule hosted a variety of experimental reactors, including the Phénix fast breeder reactor, which was operational from 1973 to 2009. The Phénix reactor was part of a broader effort to develop fast breeder technology, which was seen as a way to make more efficient use of nuclear fuel and potentially reduce the long-term environmental impact of nuclear energy.

- **Reprocessing and Waste Management:** One of the most significant aspects of the Marcoule Nuclear Site's operations has been its involvement in the reprocessing of nuclear fuel. Reprocessing is the process of separating usable fissile material, such as plutonium and uranium, from spent nuclear fuel. This material can then be reused in reactors, reducing the need for fresh uranium and helping to manage the growing stockpiles of nuclear waste. Marcoule's reprocessing activities began in earnest in the 1960s with the construction of the UP1 plant, which was used to reprocess fuel from both civilian and military reactors. Over the decades, Marcoule has processed thousands of tons of spent fuel, making it one of the key facilities in France's nuclear fuel cycle. However, reprocessing also generates significant amounts of radioactive waste, including both high-level waste (HLW) and low- and intermediate-level waste (LILW). Managing this waste has been a central challenge for the Marcoule site, and various facilities have been built to handle and store different types of radioactive material.

- **The Centraco Facility:** The Centraco facility, where the 2011 accident occurred, was specifically designed to treat and condition low- and intermediate-level radioactive waste. Centraco, operated by SOCODEI (Société pour le Conditionnement des Déchets et des Effluents Industriels), a subsidiary of EDF (Électricité de France), began operations in 1999. The facility's primary function was to process metallic and combustible waste from various nuclear sites across France, reducing its volume and preparing it for safe storage or disposal. Centraco featured two main processing units: a melting unit for metallic waste and an incineration unit for combustible waste. The melting unit was used to process metal components, such as tools, pipes, and structural materials, that had been contaminated with low levels of radioactivity. These materials were melted down, allowing the radioactive contaminants to be concentrated and separated from the bulk of the metal, which could then be recycled or disposed of as lower-level waste. The incineration unit, on the other hand, was used to burn combustible waste, such as protective clothing, plastics, and other materials that had been used in nuclear facilities. The incineration process reduced the volume of waste by up to 90%, and the resulting ash was then treated and packaged for disposal.

The 2011 Accident: Sequence of Events and Root Causes

- **Lead-Up to the Accident:** On the morning of September 12, 2011, routine operations were underway at the Centraco facility. Workers were preparing to melt a batch of metallic waste in the melting unit. The waste included various metal components that had been contaminated with low levels of radioactivity. The melting process was considered a standard procedure, and the facility had processed similar batches of waste many times before. However, unknown to the operators, the batch of waste that was being processed that day contained materials that were not suitable for the melting process. Specifically, the batch included a container that held a type of waste that, under the high temperatures of the melting furnace, could lead to a dangerous chemical reaction.

- **The Explosion:** At approximately 11:45 AM, a powerful explosion occurred in the melting unit. The explosion was caused by the rapid expansion of gases generated by the chemical reaction within the furnace. The force of the explosion was so great that it blew off the roof of the building housing the melting unit and caused significant damage to the facility's infrastructure. Tragically, one worker was killed in the explosion, and four others were injured. The explosion also released a small amount of radioactive material into the building, though fortunately, the containment systems in place at Centraco prevented any significant release of radiation into the environment.

- **Immediate Response:** The immediate response to the explosion was swift. Emergency protocols were activated, and the facility was quickly evacuated. Local fire and emergency services were called to the scene, and a perimeter was established around the site to prevent unauthorized access. The French nuclear safety authority, ASN (Autorité de Sûreté Nucléaire), was notified of the incident and immediately launched an investigation. ASN also worked with the operators of the Centraco facility to ensure that the situation was under control and that there was no risk of further explosions or radiation release. Within hours of the explosion, the site was secured, and efforts began to assess the damage and determine the cause of the accident. The initial focus was on ensuring the safety of the remaining workers and preventing any further incidents, but attention soon turned to the investigation of what had gone wrong.

Investigation and Analysis: Understanding the Root Causes

- **ASN's Investigation:** The investigation into the Centraco accident was led by ASN, with the support of other government agencies and independent experts. The investigation sought to determine the root causes of the explosion, as well as any failures in safety procedures, training, or equipment that may have contributed to the incident. One of the key findings of the investigation was that the batch of waste being processed at the time of the accident included materials that were not suitable for melting. Specifically, the waste contained traces of chlorine and other chemicals that, when exposed to the high temperatures in the furnace, led to the production of volatile gases. These gases built up inside the furnace until they reached a critical pressure, resulting in the explosion. The investigation also revealed that there were shortcomings in the facility's waste handling and sorting procedures. The materials that caused the explosion had not been properly identified or segregated before being sent to the melting unit. This oversight was a critical failure in the facility's safety protocols and highlighted the importance of rigorous waste classification and handling procedures in preventing such incidents.
- **Human Factors and Organizational Issues:** In addition to the technical causes of the accident, the investigation also examined the role of human factors and organizational issues.

It was found that there were gaps in the training and supervision of the workers at Centraco, particularly in relation to the handling of hazardous materials. The workers involved in the accident were experienced, but they had not received specific training on the risks associated with the particular type of waste that was being processed that day. Moreover, the investigation pointed to broader organizational issues within SOCODEI, the company that operated Centraco. There were indications that safety procedures were not always rigorously enforced and that there was a culture of complacency when it came to routine operations. This complacency may have contributed to the failure to properly inspect and classify the waste before it was processed.

- **Regulatory Oversight:** The investigation also raised questions about the effectiveness of regulatory oversight at the Marcoule site. While ASN had established comprehensive safety regulations for nuclear facilities, the Centraco accident revealed that these regulations were not always being fully implemented or enforced. In particular, the oversight of waste processing and handling activities was found to be insufficient, and there was a lack of regular inspections and audits to ensure compliance with safety standards. In response to the findings of the investigation, ASN issued a series of recommendations to improve safety at the Marcoule site and other nuclear facilities in France. These recommendations included stricter controls on waste classification, enhanced training for workers, and more rigorous enforcement of safety protocols.

The Aftermath: Cleanup, Legal Consequences, and Policy Changes

- **Cleanup and Recovery:** Following the explosion, the immediate priority was to clean up the site and ensure that it was safe for workers and the surrounding community. The damaged building was stabilized, and efforts were made to remove any remaining hazardous materials. The radioactive contamination inside the building was also carefully managed, with decontamination efforts focused on preventing any further release of radiation. The cleanup process was challenging and took several months to complete. During this time, the Centraco facility remained closed, and all waste processing activities were suspended. The incident also prompted a broader review of safety procedures at the Marcoule site, with a particular focus on improving waste handling and processing practices.

- **Legal and Regulatory Consequences:** The Centraco accident had significant legal and regulatory consequences. SOCODEI, the operator of the facility, faced legal action as a result of the accident. The company was charged with negligence and failure to ensure the safety of its workers. The case attracted considerable attention in France, particularly given the high-profile nature of the Marcoule site and the broader concerns about nuclear safety following the Fukushima disaster earlier that year. In 2014, SOCODEI was found guilty of negligence and was fined by the French courts. The company was also required to implement a series of corrective measures to address the safety issues identified in the investigation. These measures included a comprehensive review of waste handling procedures, enhanced training for workers, and improvements in the maintenance and operation of the facility. The Centraco accident also led to changes in France's nuclear safety regulations. ASN introduced new guidelines for the classification and handling of radioactive waste, with stricter requirements for the identification and segregation of hazardous materials. The regulator also increased its oversight of waste processing facilities, conducting more frequent inspections and audits to ensure compliance with safety standards.

- **Impact on Public Perception and Policy:** The Centraco accident occurred at a time when public concern about nuclear safety was already heightened due to the Fukushima disaster in Japan. In the wake of these events, there was a renewed debate in France about the risks and benefits of nuclear energy, with some calling for a reduction in the country's reliance on nuclear power. While the Centraco accident did not lead to a major shift in French energy policy, it did contribute to a growing awareness of the importance of safety in the nuclear industry. The incident highlighted the potential dangers associated with nuclear waste processing and underscored the need for robust safety measures to protect workers, the public, and the environment. In the years following the accident, there was also a greater emphasis on transparency and communication in the nuclear sector. The French government and regulatory authorities made efforts to improve public access to information about nuclear safety and to engage more openly with communities living near nuclear facilities.

Lessons Learned: The Broader Implications of the Marcoule Accident

- **Safety in Waste Management:** One of the key lessons from the Centraco accident is the critical importance of safety in the management of radioactive waste. The accident demonstrated that even low- and intermediate-level waste can pose significant risks if not handled properly. This underscores the need for rigorous waste classification, handling, and processing procedures, as well as continuous monitoring and oversight to ensure that these procedures are followed. The incident also highlighted the challenges associated with dealing with legacy waste, particularly in older nuclear facilities. As nuclear sites around the world continue to manage and decommission aging reactors and facilities, the safe treatment and disposal of accumulated waste will remain a key challenge.

- **Human Factors and Organizational Culture:** The Centraco accident also emphasized the role of human factors and organizational culture in nuclear safety. The investigation revealed that complacency and a lack of rigorous safety practices can lead to serious accidents, even in routine operations. This highlights the need for a strong safety culture within nuclear organizations, where safety is prioritized at all levels, and where workers are empowered to identify and address potential risks. Training and education are also critical components of a strong safety culture. The Centraco accident demonstrated the importance of ensuring that all workers, regardless of their level of experience, receive comprehensive training on the specific hazards associated with their tasks. This training should be regularly updated and reinforced to ensure that safety remains a top priority.

- **Regulatory Oversight and Public Confidence:** Finally, the Centraco accident underscored the importance of effective regulatory oversight in maintaining public confidence in nuclear energy. The incident revealed gaps in the oversight of waste processing activities at Marcoule, which contributed to the conditions that led to the explosion. This highlights the need for continuous vigilance by regulatory authorities and the importance of enforcing safety standards consistently across all nuclear facilities. The accident also demonstrated the importance of transparency and communication in the nuclear industry. Public confidence in nuclear energy depends not only on the safe operation of facilities but also on the willingness of operators and regulators to engage openly with the public and to provide clear, accurate information about risks and safety measures.

Chapter 20: Majak Disaster

The Majak Production Association, originally known as Chelyabinsk-40 and later as Chelyabinsk-65, is one of the most notorious nuclear facilities in the world, primarily due to the disaster that took place there in 1957. Located in the southern Urals, near the town of Kyshtym in the Soviet Union, the Majak facility was one of the Soviet Union's most secretive and significant nuclear production sites. It was established shortly after World War II as part of the USSR's efforts to develop nuclear weapons during the Cold War.

Majak was the centerpiece of the Soviet nuclear weapons program and played a critical role in the production of plutonium, which was essential for the creation of nuclear bombs. The facility's operations were shrouded in secrecy, and for many years, even the existence of Majak was unknown to the outside world. However, this secrecy also contributed to a lack of oversight and safety measures, ultimately leading to one of the worst nuclear accidents in history: the Majak disaster, also known as the Kyshtym disaster.

The disaster, which occurred on September 29, 1957, was the result of a massive explosion in a storage tank containing highly radioactive waste. The explosion released a large amount of radioactive material into the environment, contaminating a vast area of land and affecting thousands of people. The event is considered the third most serious nuclear accident in history, after the Chernobyl disaster in 1986 and the Fukushima disaster in 2011.

In this detailed exploration, we will examine the background of the Majak facility, the events leading up to the 1957 disaster, the explosion itself, and its immediate and long-term consequences. We will also discuss the broader implications for nuclear safety, the environment, and public health, as well as the lessons learned from this catastrophic event.

The Majak Facility: Origins and Development

- **Establishment and Early Operations:** The Majak facility was established in 1945, just after the end of World War II, as part of the Soviet Union's efforts to develop nuclear weapons. The facility was located in a remote area of the southern Urals, chosen for its relative isolation, which made it easier to maintain secrecy and control access. The construction of Majak was a massive undertaking, involving tens of thousands of workers, many of whom were prisoners or forced laborers. The facility was operational by 1948, and within a short time, it became one of the most important sites in the Soviet nuclear program. Majak's primary function was the production of weapons-grade plutonium, which was achieved through the operation of nuclear reactors that irradiated uranium fuel. The plutonium produced at Majak was then extracted and purified in a series of chemical processes, which generated large amounts of radioactive waste. This waste included both liquid and solid radioactive materials, as well as gaseous emissions. Managing this waste was a significant challenge, particularly given the secrecy and haste with which the Soviet nuclear program was pursued.

- **Secrecy and Lack of Oversight:** The secrecy surrounding the Majak facility was extreme, even by the standards of the Soviet Union. The facility was not marked on maps, and the workers and residents in the surrounding area were subject to strict controls on their movements and communications. This secrecy extended to the management of radioactive waste, which was often handled with little regard for safety or environmental impact. In the early years of operation, much of the radioactive waste produced at Majak was simply dumped into nearby rivers and lakes, including the Techa River, which flowed through several villages. This practice led to widespread contamination of the local environment and exposed thousands of people to dangerous levels of radiation. The long-term health effects of this contamination are still being felt today, with elevated rates of cancer and other radiation-related illnesses in the affected population. The lack of oversight and safety measures at Majak was symptomatic of the broader approach to nuclear development in the Soviet Union at the time. The primary focus was on rapidly producing nuclear weapons to compete with the United States, and concerns about safety, environmental protection, and public health were often subordinated to this goal.

The Events Leading Up to the 1957 Disaster

- **Increasing Levels of Radioactive Waste:** By the mid-1950s, the Majak facility was producing large amounts of radioactive waste, much of which was stored on-site in a series of underground and above-ground tanks. These tanks were used to store highly radioactive liquid waste, which was a byproduct of the chemical processes used to extract plutonium from irradiated uranium fuel. The waste in these tanks was extremely dangerous, containing high concentrations of long-lived radioactive isotopes, including strontium-90 and cesium-137. One of the key challenges in managing this waste was preventing it from overheating. The radioactive decay of the waste generated heat, which had to be dissipated to prevent the temperature inside the tanks from rising to dangerous levels. To manage this heat, the tanks were equipped with cooling systems that circulated water around the waste to remove excess heat. However, the cooling systems at Majak were poorly designed and maintained, and by 1956, several of the tanks were experiencing problems with overheating. In some cases, the cooling systems had failed altogether, leading to a dangerous buildup of heat inside the tanks.

- **Warning Signs and Ignored Risks:** In the months leading up to the disaster, there were several warning signs that the situation at Majak was deteriorating. Workers at the facility reported problems with the cooling systems, including leaks and blockages in the pipes that circulated water around the waste tanks. There were also concerns about the structural integrity of the tanks themselves, some of which had developed cracks and other signs of wear and tear. Despite these warning signs, little was done to address the underlying issues. The secrecy and pressure to maintain production levels at Majak meant that safety concerns were often ignored or downplayed. Workers who raised concerns were sometimes dismissed or transferred to other jobs, and there was a general atmosphere of complacency about the risks associated with the storage of radioactive waste. By the summer of 1957, the situation had reached a critical point. Several of the waste tanks were operating at dangerously high temperatures, and there were growing fears that a major accident was imminent. However, due to the secrecy surrounding Majak, these fears were not communicated to higher authorities in Moscow, and no action was taken to prevent the disaster that was about to unfold.

The 1957 Explosion: A Catastrophic Release of Radiation

- **The Explosion and Its Immediate Aftermath:** On September 29, 1957, at approximately 4:20 PM local time, a massive explosion occurred in one of the waste storage tanks at the Majak facility. The tank in question contained approximately 70-80 tons of highly radioactive liquid waste, and the explosion was caused by the buildup of heat and pressure inside the tank. The explosion had the force of about 70-100 tons of TNT and completely destroyed the tank, sending a plume of radioactive material high into the atmosphere. The explosion released an estimated 20 million curies (740 petabecquerels) of radioactive material into the environment, including large amounts of strontium-90, cesium-137, and other long-lived radioactive isotopes. The radioactive plume was carried by the wind in a northeasterly direction, contaminating a large area of land across the southern Urals. The most heavily affected area, known as the East-Ural Radioactive Trace (EURT), covered approximately 20,000 square kilometers. The immediate aftermath of the explosion was chaotic and confused. The blast was heard for miles around, and a cloud of radioactive dust was visible in the sky above the Majak facility. However, due to the secrecy surrounding the site, local residents were not informed of the nature of the disaster or the dangers they faced. Many people continued with their daily activities, unaware that they were being exposed to dangerous levels of radiation.

- **Evacuation and Containment Efforts:** In the days following the explosion, the Soviet authorities began to organize a response to the disaster. However, the response was slow and inadequate, largely due to the secrecy and lack of preparedness for such an event. The first priority was to contain the spread of radioactive contamination and to evacuate the most heavily affected areas. Evacuations began several days after the explosion, but they were poorly coordinated and often came too late to protect people from the worst of the radiation exposure. Approximately 10,000 people were eventually evacuated from their homes, but many others were left behind in contaminated areas. The evacuations were carried out with little explanation, and the evacuees were often resettled in distant locations without adequate support or compensation. In addition to the evacuations, efforts were made to decontaminate the affected areas. This involved the removal of topsoil, the destruction of contaminated buildings and crops, and the construction of new containment structures at the Majak site. However, these efforts were limited in scope and effectiveness, and much of the contaminated area remained dangerously radioactive for decades.

- **Health and Environmental Impact:** The health and environmental impact of the Majak disaster was severe and long-lasting. The initial explosion and the subsequent release of radiation exposed thousands of people to high levels of radiation, leading to an increase in cancer rates, birth defects, and other radiation-related illnesses in the affected population. The contaminated area, known as the EURT, became one of the most polluted places on Earth. The soil, water, and vegetation in the region were heavily contaminated with radioactive isotopes, and the area remained hazardous for many years. Even today, parts of the EURT are still uninhabitable, and the long-term environmental impact of the disaster continues to be felt. The full extent of the health impact of the Majak disaster is difficult to determine, in part because of the secrecy that surrounded the event. For many years, the Soviet authorities denied that the disaster had occurred, and information about the incident was only made public in the 1980s, following the Chernobyl disaster. As a result, many of the people affected by the Majak disaster were never properly diagnosed or treated for their radiation exposure.

The Aftermath: Secrecy, Denial, and the Search for Justice

- **Soviet Secrecy and Denial:** In the immediate aftermath of the Majak disaster, the Soviet authorities imposed strict secrecy on all information related to the event. The disaster was not reported in the Soviet press, and the affected area was designated as a closed zone, with access restricted to those with special permits. The evacuated villages were erased from maps, and the residents who were relocated were instructed not to speak about the events they had witnessed. For many years, the Soviet government denied that any major nuclear accident had occurred at Majak. The official explanation for the evacuations and the contamination was that they were the result of routine industrial activities. It was not until the 1980s, after the Chernobyl disaster drew international attention to the issue of nuclear safety in the Soviet Union, that the true nature of the Majak disaster began to emerge.

- **International Awareness and Response:** The first international reports of the Majak disaster appeared in the late 1970s, based on information from Soviet dissidents and defectors. These reports described a major nuclear accident in the southern Urals, but the details were vague and often contradictory. It was not until 1986, following the Chernobyl disaster, that the Soviet authorities finally acknowledged that a major nuclear accident had occurred at Majak in 1957. The international response to the Majak disaster was mixed. On the one hand, the disaster highlighted the dangers of nuclear energy and the need for greater transparency and safety measures in the nuclear industry. On the other hand, the secrecy surrounding the event made it difficult for international organizations and governments to assess the full impact of the disaster and to provide assistance to the affected population.

- **Legal and Moral Responsibility:** In the years since the Majak disaster, there have been efforts to seek justice and compensation for the people affected by the event. However, these efforts have been hampered by the lack of information about the disaster and the ongoing secrecy surrounding the Majak facility. In the 1990s, after the collapse of the Soviet Union, some survivors of the Majak disaster began to speak out about their experiences and to demand compensation for their injuries and losses. These efforts have had limited success, with only a small number of people receiving compensation or recognition for the harm they suffered. The Majak disaster also raises important questions about the moral responsibility of governments and corporations in the management of nuclear technology. The disaster was the result of a combination of technical failures, human error, and a culture of secrecy and denial that prioritized the pursuit of nuclear weapons over the safety and well-being of people and the environment.

Lessons Learned: The Legacy of the Majak Disaster

- **Nuclear Safety and Transparency:** The Majak disaster is a powerful reminder of the importance of safety and transparency in the nuclear industry. The disaster was caused in large part by the secrecy and lack of oversight that characterized the Soviet nuclear program, and it underscores the need for rigorous safety measures and open communication in the management of nuclear facilities. One of the key lessons of the Majak disaster is the importance of proper waste management in the nuclear industry. The explosion was triggered by the failure to properly manage the heat generated by radioactive waste, and it highlights the need for robust systems to safely store and dispose of nuclear waste. This lesson is particularly relevant today, as the world continues to grapple with the challenges of nuclear waste disposal and the risks associated with aging nuclear facilities.

- **Environmental and Health Impacts:** The long-term environmental and health impacts of the Majak disaster also offer important lessons for the future. The disaster contaminated a vast area of land and exposed thousands of people to dangerous levels of radiation, leading to long-term health problems and environmental degradation. These impacts underscore the need for comprehensive monitoring and remediation efforts in the aftermath of nuclear accidents, as well as the importance of providing adequate medical care and support to affected populations. The Majak disaster also highlights the need for ongoing research into the health effects of radiation exposure. The lack of information about the long-term health impacts of the disaster has made it difficult to fully understand the consequences of the event, and it underscores the importance of continued research and monitoring in this area.

- **Ethical and Moral Considerations:** Finally, the Majak disaster raises important ethical and moral questions about the use of nuclear technology. The disaster was the result of a combination of technical failures, human error, and a culture of secrecy and denial that prioritized the pursuit of nuclear weapons over the safety and well-being of people and the environment. This raises important questions about the ethical responsibilities of governments and corporations in the management of nuclear technology, and it underscores the need for a more responsible and transparent approach to the use of nuclear energy.

Chapter 21: Andreev Bay Nuclear Waste Storage Incidents

Andreev Bay, a remote and frigid inlet on the Kola Peninsula in Russia's far northwest, is a site steeped in the Cold War's dark history. Located near the Barents Sea, this isolated area was once a pivotal part of the Soviet Union's extensive nuclear submarine fleet operations. Today, however, Andreev Bay is better known for the environmental and radiological dangers posed by the remnants of its past—a legacy of nuclear waste and radiological contamination that has haunted the region for decades.

The site was originally established in the 1960s as a storage and maintenance facility for the Soviet Northern Fleet's nuclear submarines. This facility was critical for the fleet, serving as a hub where spent nuclear fuel and radioactive waste from submarines were stored, awaiting processing or disposal. During the height of the Cold War, the Soviet Union operated a large number of nuclear submarines, many of which were stationed in the Barents Sea. Andreev Bay played a crucial role in maintaining the operational readiness of these submarines, handling significant quantities of radioactive material in the process.

However, the rapid expansion of the Soviet Navy and the intense pressure of the arms race led to the establishment of facilities like Andreev Bay with little regard for long-term environmental safety. The lack of proper infrastructure for the secure storage of radioactive materials, combined with the harsh Arctic conditions and the secrecy surrounding military operations, created a situation ripe for disaster.

Over the decades, Andreev Bay has become synonymous with nuclear waste mismanagement and environmental contamination. The facility's deteriorating condition, coupled with numerous incidents involving radioactive leaks and accidents, has made it one of the most significant nuclear waste storage concerns in the world. The story of Andreev Bay is not just one of historical interest but also of ongoing environmental challenges and international efforts to mitigate the risks associated with this dangerous legacy.

The Establishment of Andreev Bay: A Hub for Nuclear Submarine Operations

- **The Strategic Importance of the Kola Peninsula:** The Kola Peninsula, where Andreev Bay is located, has long been of strategic importance to Russia, primarily due to its proximity to the Arctic and the North Atlantic. During the Cold War, the Kola Peninsula became one of the most militarized regions in the world, home to numerous naval bases, airfields, and other military installations. The Soviet Northern Fleet, headquartered in Severomorsk, relied heavily on the facilities in this region to support its operations. Andreev Bay was chosen as a site for nuclear waste storage and submarine maintenance due to its remote location and the natural protection offered by the surrounding terrain. The bay provided a sheltered harbor where submarines could dock, and the nearby facilities allowed for the transfer and storage of spent nuclear fuel and other radioactive materials.

- **The Cold War Nuclear Arms Race:** The 1960s and 1970s saw a dramatic increase in the number of nuclear-powered submarines in the Soviet Navy. These submarines, equipped with ballistic missiles and capable of remaining submerged for extended periods, were a key component of the Soviet Union's nuclear deterrent strategy. As the number of submarines grew, so too did the need for facilities to handle the radioactive waste generated by their reactors. Andreev Bay was rapidly developed to meet this need. The facility included storage pools for spent nuclear fuel, warehouses for radioactive waste, and docks for the maintenance and refueling of submarines. However, the focus on rapid development and the intense secrecy surrounding the site meant that safety and environmental considerations were often overlooked. The construction of Andreev Bay was carried out with little regard for the long-term implications of storing large quantities of radioactive material in a harsh Arctic environment. The storage facilities were not designed to last indefinitely, and the infrastructure was often inadequate to safely contain the radioactive materials. This lack of foresight would have serious consequences in the years to come.

The Deterioration of Andreev Bay: Decades of Neglect and Radioactive Contamination

- **Post-Cold War Decline:** The collapse of the Soviet Union in 1991 marked the beginning of a period of significant decline for many of the military installations in the former Soviet states, and Andreev Bay was no exception. With the end of the Cold War, the Russian Navy faced severe budget cuts, and many of the Northern Fleet's facilities, including Andreev Bay, were abandoned or left to deteriorate. The infrastructure at Andreev Bay, already aging and poorly maintained, began to crumble. The storage pools and warehouses at Andreev Bay were originally intended to be temporary solutions for the storage of nuclear waste. However, with the dissolution of the Soviet Union, the plans for the removal and safe disposal of this waste were largely abandoned. As a result, vast quantities of spent nuclear fuel and other radioactive materials were left in aging, inadequately maintained facilities, exposed to the harsh Arctic environment.

- **Environmental and Radiological Risks:** The deterioration of Andreev Bay's infrastructure has led to significant environmental and radiological risks. The storage pools, which were designed to hold spent nuclear fuel rods underwater to prevent them from overheating, began to leak due to corrosion and structural damage. The warehouses where solid radioactive waste was stored also deteriorated, leading to the release of radioactive dust and contamination of the surrounding area. One of the most significant risks associated with Andreev Bay is the potential for a catastrophic release of radiation into the environment. The spent nuclear fuel stored at the site contains large amounts of highly radioactive materials, including plutonium and uranium. If these materials were to be released due to a structural failure or other accident, it could lead to widespread contamination of the Barents Sea and the surrounding region. In addition to the risk of a major accident, the ongoing leakage of radioactive materials from the site has led to the gradual contamination of the environment. The soil, water, and vegetation around Andreev Bay are all contaminated with radioactive isotopes, posing a long-term threat to the health of the local ecosystem and the people who live in the region.

- **Human Health Concerns:** The radiological contamination at Andreev Bay has also raised significant concerns about the health of the people who have worked at or lived near the site. The workers who handled the radioactive materials at Andreev Bay were often poorly trained and lacked adequate protective equipment, leading to high levels of radiation exposure. Many of these workers have suffered from radiation-related illnesses, including cancer, and the long-term health effects on the local population remain a serious concern. The local communities in the region have also been affected by the contamination. Although Andreev Bay is located in a remote area, the contamination has spread to nearby water sources and agricultural land, raising concerns about the safety of the local food supply. The potential for long-term health effects, including increased rates of cancer and other radiation-related illnesses, is a significant issue for the people living near Andreev Bay.

The Incidents: A History of Accidents and Near-Misses

- **1979 Incident: Leakage of Radioactive Material:** One of the earliest and most significant incidents at Andreev Bay occurred in 1979 when a significant amount of radioactive material leaked from one of the storage pools. The incident was the result of a combination of factors, including poor maintenance of the storage pool, inadequate monitoring of the facility, and a lack of proper safety protocols. The leak led to the contamination of the surrounding area, including the soil and groundwater. The Soviet authorities attempted to contain the contamination by constructing a temporary barrier around the affected area, but the leak was never fully controlled. The incident was kept secret for many years, and the full extent of the contamination was not revealed until much later.

- **1982 Explosion: A Near-Miss Catastrophe:** In 1982, a significant explosion occurred in one of the storage facilities at Andreev Bay. The explosion was caused by the accumulation of hydrogen gas in a storage tank containing radioactive waste. The gas had built up due to the decomposition of organic materials in the waste, and the explosion was triggered by a spark. The explosion caused significant damage to the storage facility, but fortunately, it did not lead to a major release of radiation. However, the incident highlighted the poor condition of the storage facilities at Andreev Bay and the lack of adequate safety measures. The explosion was another in a series of near-miss incidents that underscored the precarious situation at the site.

- **1994 Incident: Submarine Accident and Fuel Rod Spill:** In 1994, a serious accident occurred during the refueling of a nuclear submarine at Andreev Bay. During the operation, a spent fuel rod was accidentally dropped, leading to the release of radioactive material. The incident was caused by a combination of human error and the poor condition of the equipment used in the refueling process. The spill led to the contamination of the dock area and the surrounding waters. Although the incident did not result in a major release of radiation, it highlighted the ongoing risks associated with the handling of nuclear materials at Andreev Bay. The accident also raised concerns about the safety of the submarines themselves, many of which were aging and in poor condition.

- **Ongoing Leaks and Structural Failures:** In addition to these specific incidents, Andreev Bay has been plagued by ongoing leaks and structural failures. The storage pools, which were never designed to hold nuclear waste for decades, have continued to deteriorate, leading to frequent leaks of radioactive water. The warehouses where solid waste is stored have also suffered from structural damage, leading to the release of radioactive dust. These ongoing issues have made it difficult to fully assess the extent of the contamination at Andreev Bay. The site is a patchwork of makeshift repairs and containment efforts, and the full scale of the radiological risk is not well understood. The continued degradation of the infrastructure at Andreev Bay poses a significant challenge to efforts to secure and clean up the site.

International Response and Cleanup Efforts: Addressing the Legacy of Andreev Bay

- **International Concern and Collaboration:** The ongoing radiological risks at Andreev Bay have drawn significant international attention, particularly from neighboring countries in Scandinavia and other Arctic nations. The potential for a major release of radioactive material into the Barents Sea and the Arctic Ocean has raised concerns about the environmental and health impacts on a global scale. In response to these concerns, international organizations and governments have been involved in efforts to address the situation at Andreev Bay. The International Atomic Energy Agency (IAEA) has played a key role in assessing the radiological risks at the site and providing technical assistance for the cleanup and remediation efforts. Countries like Norway, which shares a border with the Kola Peninsula, have also provided financial and technical support to help secure the site and prevent further contamination. The European Bank for Reconstruction and Development (EBRD) has been involved in funding projects aimed at improving the safety of the storage facilities at Andreev Bay. These projects have included efforts to repair and reinforce the aging storage pools, construct new containment structures, and improve the monitoring and management of the radioactive waste at the site. The goal of these efforts is to reduce the immediate risks posed by the deteriorating infrastructure and to create a safer environment for the eventual removal and disposal of the nuclear waste.

- **Challenges and Progress in Cleanup Efforts:** The cleanup and remediation of Andreev Bay have been a complex and challenging process. The site is remote, and the harsh Arctic conditions make it difficult to carry out work for much of the year. The infrastructure at the site is in such poor condition that even basic tasks like moving equipment or conducting inspections can be hazardous. One of the primary challenges has been the removal of the spent nuclear fuel from the storage pools. These fuel rods are highly radioactive and must be handled with extreme care to avoid a catastrophic release of radiation. The removal process has been slow and painstaking, with each fuel rod needing to be carefully extracted and safely transported to a more secure facility. In addition to the technical challenges, there have also been significant logistical and financial hurdles to overcome. The cleanup efforts at Andreev Bay are expensive, and funding has been limited. The international community has provided support, but the sheer scale of the problem has made it difficult to secure the necessary resources to fully address the situation. Despite these challenges, there has been some progress in the cleanup efforts. Several of the most severely damaged storage facilities have been reinforced, and the removal of spent nuclear fuel has begun. However, much work remains to be done, and the long-term safety of Andreev Bay is still uncertain.

The Future of Andreev Bay: A Cautionary Tale for Nuclear Waste Management

- **Ongoing Risks and the Need for Vigilance:** The story of Andreev Bay is far from over. The site remains one of the most hazardous nuclear waste storage facilities in the world, and the risks posed by the deteriorating infrastructure and ongoing contamination are still very real. The cleanup efforts at Andreev Bay are a long-term project that will require ongoing vigilance and support from the international community. One of the key lessons of Andreev Bay is the importance of proper nuclear waste management. The situation at Andreev Bay is the result of decades of neglect and the failure to adequately plan for the long-term storage of radioactive materials. The consequences of this neglect are still being felt today, and they serve as a powerful reminder of the dangers of mismanaging nuclear waste.

- **Lessons for the Global Nuclear Industry:** The challenges faced at Andreev Bay are not unique. Around the world, there are many other sites where nuclear waste is stored in aging or inadequate facilities. The lessons of Andreev Bay are therefore relevant to the global nuclear industry, which must grapple with the long-term management of nuclear waste and the risks associated with aging infrastructure. One of the most important lessons is the need for transparency and international cooperation in dealing with nuclear waste. The secrecy that surrounded Andreev Bay during the Cold War contributed to the current situation, as the true scale of the problem was hidden for many years. Today, the international community must work together to ensure that similar situations do not arise elsewhere and that nuclear waste is managed in a safe and responsible manner.

- **A Call to Action:** The ongoing situation at Andreev Bay is a call to action for governments, international organizations, and the nuclear industry as a whole. The risks posed by the site are a stark reminder of the dangers of nuclear technology and the need for rigorous safety standards and long-term planning. The story of Andreev Bay is not just a historical footnote but a pressing issue that demands attention and action.

Chapter 22: K-19 Nuclear Submarine Accident

The K-19 nuclear submarine, one of the Soviet Union's first ballistic missile submarines, has become infamous for its association with one of the most harrowing nuclear accidents in naval history. The story of K-19 is not just a tale of technological failure and human suffering, but also a reflection of the intense pressures and perils of the Cold War era.

Constructed as part of the Soviet Union's ambitious efforts to compete with the United States in the nuclear arms race, K-19 was rushed into service in 1961, symbolizing the Soviet Union's determination to maintain nuclear parity. However, the submarine's tragic accident in July 1961, just a few months after its commissioning, would expose the dangers inherent in this rush to nuclear power and the immense human cost that could result from technical failures and the harsh realities of Cold War geopolitics.

The Genesis of K-19: Ambition and Secrecy

- **The Soviet Union's Nuclear Ambitions:** The end of World War II and the dawn of the Cold War saw the United States and the Soviet Union locked in a tense and dangerous competition for global supremacy. Central to this rivalry was the development of nuclear weapons and the means to deliver them. The launch of the first Soviet nuclear-powered submarine, K-3, in 1958 marked a significant milestone in the Soviet Navy's ability to project power globally. However, the Soviet leadership, led by Premier Nikita Khrushchev, was determined to go further and develop a fleet of ballistic missile submarines capable of delivering nuclear strikes from beneath the ocean's surface. The K-19 was conceived as part of this ambitious plan. The submarine was designed to carry R-13 ballistic missiles, which could be launched from underwater and reach targets thousands of kilometers away. The development of the K-19 was a top priority for the Soviet Navy, and the submarine was rushed into production under intense pressure to match and surpass American capabilities.

- **The Construction of K-19:** The construction of K-19 began in October 1958 at the Severodvinsk shipyard in northern Russia. The project was marked by urgency and secrecy, with engineers and workers laboring under tight deadlines and immense pressure to complete the submarine as quickly as possible. The K-19 was the lead vessel of the Soviet Navy's first series of ballistic missile submarines, known as Project 658, or Hotel-class submarines. The design and construction of K-19 were fraught with challenges. The submarine was equipped with two nuclear reactors to power its propulsion system, a relatively new and complex technology at the time. The reactors were designed to provide the submarine with the ability to remain submerged for extended periods, making it a formidable strategic weapon. However, the rush to complete K-19 meant that many aspects of the design and construction were not thoroughly tested, and numerous technical problems were overlooked or inadequately addressed.
- **The "Widowmaker": Early Signs of Trouble:** Even before its catastrophic accident in 1961, K-19 had earned a reputation as an ill-fated vessel. The submarine experienced several serious incidents during its construction and early trials, including electrical fires, leaks, and mechanical failures. These problems led to delays in the submarine's commissioning, but the urgency of the Cold War meant that K-19 was pushed into service despite these issues. The crew of K-19, many of whom were young and inexperienced, were well aware of the

submarine's problematic history. The vessel's ominous nickname, "Hiroshima," reflected the crew's fears of the dangers posed by the submarine's nuclear reactors. These fears would prove tragically well-founded.

The 1961 Accident: A Crisis Unfolds Beneath the Sea

- **Setting the Stage: The Mission of K-19:** On July 4, 1961, K-19 was on a routine patrol in the North Atlantic, part of a broader mission to test the submarine's capabilities and readiness for potential conflict. The submarine was operating at a depth of 100 meters, with its crew of 139 men conducting standard procedures and drills. The mission was a critical part of the Soviet Union's strategy to demonstrate its nuclear deterrent capability and maintain pressure on the United States during a period of heightened Cold War tensions. The crew of K-19 was composed of a mix of experienced sailors and young recruits, many of whom had never served on a nuclear submarine before. The captain, Nikolai Zateyev, was an experienced officer who had served in the Soviet Navy for many years, but even he could not have anticipated the crisis that was about to unfold.

- **The Reactor Malfunction: A Deadly Crisis Emerges:** At approximately 0400 hours on July 4, 1961, alarms began to sound in the reactor control room of K-19. The crew quickly discovered that the submarine's primary cooling system for one of the reactors had failed. The reactor's temperature began to rise rapidly, creating a critical situation that could lead to a catastrophic meltdown and the release of radioactive materials. The failure of the cooling system was later attributed to a manufacturing defect in the reactor's coolant pipes. The defect had gone unnoticed during the submarine's construction and early trials, and the rushed nature of the project meant that proper safety measures and redundancies were not in place. As the reactor's temperature continued to rise, the crew faced the very real possibility of a nuclear disaster that could not only destroy the submarine but also have far-reaching consequences for the surrounding environment and potentially spark a larger conflict.

- **The Crew's Response: Heroism in the Face of Disaster:** In the face of this escalating crisis, Captain Zateyev made the decision to surface the submarine, hoping to gain access to fresh air and buy time to address the reactor malfunction. However, the situation was dire, and the crew quickly realized that they had no way to repair the cooling system using the equipment on board. Faced with the prospect of a reactor meltdown, Captain Zateyev ordered a group of eight crew members to enter the reactor compartment and manually rig a temporary cooling system. This involved creating a makeshift coolant circuit by cutting pipes and welding them together, all while being exposed to lethal levels of radiation. The crew members who undertook this task knew that they were sacrificing their lives to save their shipmates and prevent a larger catastrophe. The work of these men was nothing short of heroic. Despite the extreme heat and the intense radiation, they succeeded in rigging a temporary cooling system that stabilized the reactor and prevented a meltdown. However, the radiation exposure they endured was fatal. Within days, all eight crew members had succumbed to acute radiation sickness, suffering excruciating deaths as a result of their selfless actions.

- **The Aftermath: Rescue and Return to Port:** With the reactor stabilized, K-19 remained adrift in the North Atlantic for several hours, unable to move due to the reactor malfunction. The crew sent out distress signals, but the submarine was in a remote location, and the nearest Soviet vessels were several hundred kilometers away. The situation was further complicated by the presence of NATO forces in the area, who were closely monitoring Soviet submarine activity. After several hours, a Soviet diesel-powered submarine, S-270, responded to K-19's distress signals and arrived on the scene. The crew of K-19 was transferred to S-270, and the stricken submarine was towed back to its home port at Severomorsk. The entire operation took several days, during which time the remaining crew members of K-19 were exposed to additional radiation, although not at the lethal levels experienced by the reactor repair team. Upon their return to port, the surviving crew members were subjected to decontamination procedures and medical examinations. The full extent of the radiation exposure was not immediately apparent, but many crew members began to show symptoms of radiation sickness in the days and weeks following the accident.

The Human Cost: The Toll of Radiation and Secrecy

- **The Immediate Impact on the Crew:** The crew members who had been exposed to radiation during the K-19 accident suffered a range of symptoms, including nausea, vomiting, skin burns, and hair loss. Those who had been closest to the reactor compartment, including the repair team, experienced the most severe symptoms and were quickly hospitalized. Despite the best efforts of medical personnel, all eight members of the repair team died within weeks of the accident. For the surviving crew members, the psychological impact of the accident was profound. Many had witnessed the deaths of their comrades and were acutely aware of the dangers they had faced. The sense of loss and trauma was compounded by the secrecy surrounding the incident. The Soviet government, keen to maintain the illusion of infallibility, imposed strict controls on information about the accident, and the crew members were forbidden from discussing what had happened, even with their families.

- **Long-Term Health Consequences:** The long-term health effects of the K-19 accident were severe for many of the surviving crew members. Radiation exposure, even at lower levels, can lead to a range of health problems, including cancer, cardiovascular disease, and reproductive issues. In the years following the accident, many of the crew members developed cancers and other serious health conditions, which they attributed to their exposure during the K-19 incident. However, because of the secrecy surrounding the accident, many crew members struggled to receive adequate medical care or compensation. The Soviet government did not officially acknowledge the full extent of the radiation exposure, and many crew members were left to cope with their health problems on their own. It was only after the collapse of the Soviet Union that some of the crew members began to receive recognition and compensation for their suffering.

- **The Burden of Secrecy:** The Soviet government's decision to keep the K-19 accident secret had far-reaching consequences for the crew members and their families. The crew was sworn to secrecy and warned that any discussion of the incident would be considered treasonous. As a result, many crew members were unable to share their experiences with anyone, leading to a sense of isolation and alienation. The secrecy also extended to the broader Soviet public, who were kept in the dark about the dangers posed by the Soviet nuclear submarine fleet. The K-19 accident was not the only incident of its kind, but the Soviet government systematically suppressed information about these accidents, leaving the public unaware of the risks associated with the nuclear arms race.

The Legacy of K-19: Reflections on Nuclear Safety and Human Cost

- **The Lessons of K-19:** The K-19 accident highlighted the dangers of nuclear technology and the high human cost of the Cold War arms race. The incident exposed the vulnerabilities of the Soviet Union's nuclear submarine program, particularly the risks associated with rushing complex technologies into service without adequate testing and safety measures. One of the key lessons of K-19 is the importance of rigorous safety standards and oversight in the development and operation of nuclear technology. The reactor malfunction on K-19 was the result of a manufacturing defect that could have been detected and corrected if proper quality control measures had been in place. The lack of redundancy in the submarine's cooling system also contributed to the severity of the crisis, as there was no backup system to prevent the reactor from overheating. The heroism of the K-19 crew also underscores the importance of leadership and the willingness of individuals to take extraordinary risks to protect others. The actions of the repair team, who sacrificed their lives to prevent a nuclear disaster, are a testament to the bravery and selflessness that can emerge in the face of extreme danger.

- **The Impact on Soviet and Russian Naval Policy:** The K-19 accident had a significant impact on Soviet naval policy and the development of future nuclear submarines. The incident prompted a review of safety procedures and led to changes in the design of subsequent submarine classes to improve the reliability of reactor cooling systems and other critical components. However, the secrecy surrounding the K-19 accident also meant that the full lessons of the incident were not widely disseminated within the Soviet Navy. Other nuclear submarine accidents occurred in the following years, including the loss of K-129 in 1968 and K-278 Komsomolets in 1989, which highlighted ongoing challenges in the Soviet Union's nuclear submarine program. In the post-Soviet era, the Russian Navy has continued to operate a fleet of nuclear submarines, but the legacy of accidents like K-19 has influenced a more cautious approach to nuclear safety. The Russian government has also been more open about the risks associated with its nuclear submarine fleet, although concerns about transparency and accountability remain.

- **The K-19 Story in Popular Culture:** The story of K-19 has captured the public imagination and has been the subject of books, documentaries, and a major Hollywood film. The 2002 movie "K-19: The Widowmaker," directed by Kathryn Bigelow and starring Harrison Ford and Liam Neeson, brought the story of K-19 to a global audience. The film dramatizes the events of the 1961 accident, focusing on the heroism of the crew and the intense pressure faced by Captain Zateyev as he struggled to save his men and prevent a nuclear disaster. While the film takes some artistic liberties, it remains one of the most well-known portrayals of the K-19 incident and has helped to raise awareness of the dangers of nuclear technology and the human cost of the Cold War.

- **The Legacy of the K-19 Crew:** For the surviving crew members of K-19, the legacy of the accident is one of both pride and sorrow. They take pride in the bravery and sacrifice of their comrades, but they also bear the burden of the trauma and loss they experienced. In recent years, there have been efforts to honor the memory of the K-19 crew, including memorials and ceremonies recognizing their heroism. The story of K-19 serves as a powerful reminder of the human cost of the nuclear arms race and the importance of safety, transparency, and accountability in the operation of nuclear technology. It is a legacy that continues to resonate, not only in Russia but around the world, as nations grapple with the challenges of nuclear power and the lessons of the past.

Chapter 23: Hanford Nuclear Site Incidents

The Hanford Nuclear Site, located in Washington State along the Columbia River, is one of the most complex and hazardous nuclear sites in the world. Established as part of the Manhattan Project during World War II, Hanford played a critical role in the development of the United States' nuclear arsenal. However, the site is also infamous for its long history of environmental contamination, safety lapses, and accidents, many of which have had profound consequences for public health and the environment.

The Hanford Site was initially selected in 1942 due to its remote location, abundant water supply from the Columbia River, and the availability of hydroelectric power from the nearby Grand Coulee Dam. The site was tasked with producing plutonium, a key component in nuclear weapons, and by 1944, the first of Hanford's reactors, the B Reactor, was operational. The plutonium produced at Hanford was used in the Trinity test, the world's first nuclear explosion, and in the bomb dropped on Nagasaki, Japan, in August 1945.

As the Cold War intensified, Hanford expanded its operations, eventually housing nine nuclear reactors and five large plutonium processing complexes. Over four decades, the site produced the majority of the plutonium used in the U.S. nuclear arsenal. However, the rush to produce nuclear material during wartime, combined with a lack of understanding of the long-term environmental impacts, led to widespread contamination and a series of incidents that have left a lasting legacy.

The Early Years: Secrecy, Speed, and Environmental Neglect

- **The Manhattan Project Era:** The establishment of the

Hanford Site was driven by the urgency of World War II and the need to develop nuclear weapons before Nazi Germany. The Manhattan Project, under the direction of the U.S. Army Corps of Engineers, prioritized speed and secrecy above all else. The B Reactor, the world's first full-scale plutonium production reactor, was built in just 13 months, a remarkable engineering feat. However, the haste with which Hanford was developed came at a cost. During the early years of Hanford's operation, there was little understanding of the environmental and health impacts of radiation and radioactive waste. Waste from the plutonium production process, including highly radioactive liquids, was discharged directly into the ground, the Columbia River, and storage tanks, with little regard for future consequences. The secrecy surrounding the Manhattan Project meant that few outside the site were aware of the scale of the operations or the potential dangers.

- **The Cold War Expansion:** With the onset of the Cold War, Hanford's mission expanded dramatically. The Soviet Union's successful detonation of an atomic bomb in 1949 spurred the United States to ramp up its nuclear weapons production, and Hanford became a central part of this effort. New reactors and processing facilities were built, and the site operated around the clock to produce the plutonium needed for the growing U.S. nuclear arsenal. The rapid expansion of Hanford's facilities exacerbated the environmental and safety issues that had been present since the site's inception. By the 1950s, Hanford's operations were generating vast quantities of radioactive waste, much of which was stored in underground tanks or discharged into the environment. The reactors themselves, many of which were based on the original B Reactor design, were prone to leaks and other safety problems.

The Incidents: A Catalog of Contamination and Accidents

- **The Green Run (1949):** One of the earliest and most significant incidents at Hanford occurred in December 1949, in an event that would later become known as the "Green Run." The Green Run was a secret test conducted by the U.S. Air Force and the Atomic Energy Commission (AEC) to measure the dispersion of radioactive iodine-131 released from the site. The test involved processing a batch of uranium fuel that had only been cooled for 16 days, rather than the standard 83 days, leading to a much higher release of radioactive iodine. The release, which was estimated to be 8,000 curies of iodine-131, spread over a wide area, including populated regions downwind from Hanford. The Green Run was not made public until decades later, and the full extent of the health impacts on local populations remains unclear. However, it is known that exposure to iodine-131 can increase the risk of thyroid cancer, particularly in children. The Green Run is often cited as one of the earliest examples of the U.S. government's willingness to conduct dangerous experiments on its own citizens without their knowledge or consent.

- **Tank Leaks and the Legacy of High-Level Waste:** The production of plutonium at Hanford generated large quantities of high-level radioactive waste, much of which was stored in underground tanks. By the late 1960s, Hanford had accumulated more than 50 million gallons of liquid radioactive waste, stored in 177 tanks, many of which were single-shell tanks prone to leakage. The first confirmed leak occurred in 1956, and by the 1970s, it was clear that many of the tanks were failing, allowing radioactive waste to seep into the soil and groundwater. The tank leaks at Hanford represent one of the most serious environmental challenges associated with the site. The radioactive waste in the tanks contains a complex mixture of isotopes, including cesium-137, strontium-90, and plutonium-239, which pose long-term risks to human health and the environment. The leaked waste has already contaminated the groundwater beneath Hanford, and there are concerns that it could eventually reach the Columbia River, threatening the water supply for millions of people. Efforts to address the tank leaks and stabilize the waste have been ongoing for decades, but progress has been slow, and the scale of the problem is immense. The tanks are aging, and many are well past their expected lifespan, increasing the risk of further leaks. The U.S. Department of Energy (DOE), which now oversees Hanford, has embarked on a massive cleanup effort, but the complexity and cost of the project mean that it will likely take many more decades to complete.

- **The PUREX Tunnel Collapse (2017):** In May 2017, a portion of a tunnel at Hanford's Plutonium Uranium Extraction (PUREX) Plant collapsed, raising concerns about the potential release of radioactive material. The tunnel, which was constructed in the 1950s, was used to store contaminated equipment and other radioactive waste. The collapse occurred in a remote area of the site, and no workers were injured, but the incident highlighted the ongoing risks associated with Hanford's aging infrastructure. The collapse of the PUREX tunnel was a stark reminder of the challenges posed by Hanford's legacy of contamination. The site contains a vast network of aging buildings, tunnels, and storage facilities, many of which are in poor condition and pose significant safety risks. The incident prompted a renewed focus on the need to stabilize and decommission these structures to prevent future accidents.

- **Groundwater Contamination and the Risk to the**

Columbia River: The contamination of groundwater at Hanford is one of the most pressing environmental issues associated with the site. Over the decades of operation, large quantities of radioactive and hazardous chemicals have leaked into the soil and groundwater, creating extensive contamination plumes. These plumes contain a variety of contaminants, including tritium, uranium, technetium-99, and chromium, which have the potential to migrate towards the Columbia River. The Columbia River is a vital waterway that provides drinking water, irrigation, and hydroelectric power to millions of people in the Pacific Northwest. The potential for contamination of the river is a major concern, as even low levels of radioactive contamination could have serious ecological and health impacts. The DOE has implemented a series of measures to monitor and mitigate the spread of groundwater contamination, including the installation of extraction wells and treatment systems, but the long-term effectiveness of these measures is uncertain.

- **Worker Safety Incidents and Health Risks:** The legacy of contamination at Hanford has also posed significant risks to the workers tasked with cleaning up the site. Over the years, there have been numerous incidents involving worker exposure to hazardous materials, including radioactive contamination, chemical vapors, and asbestos. These incidents have raised concerns about the safety of the cleanup operations and the health of the workers involved. One of the most persistent problems at Hanford has been the release of chemical vapors from the underground storage tanks. Workers have reported symptoms such as headaches, dizziness, and respiratory problems after being exposed to these vapors, which contain a mixture of toxic chemicals. Despite efforts to improve safety measures, vapor exposures continue to be a problem, and many workers have suffered long-term health effects as a result. The health risks associated with working at Hanford have led to numerous lawsuits and calls for better protection and compensation for workers. In 2019, the state of Washington passed a law making it easier for Hanford workers to qualify for workers' compensation if they develop certain illnesses linked to their work at the site.

The Cleanup Effort: Challenges, Progress, and Setbacks

- **The Tri-Party Agreement and the Beginning of Cleanup:** In 1989, the DOE, the Environmental Protection Agency (EPA), and the Washington State Department of Ecology signed the Hanford Federal Facility Agreement and Consent Order, commonly known as the Tri-Party Agreement. This agreement established a framework for the cleanup of the Hanford Site and set legally binding milestones for the DOE to meet in its efforts to address the contamination and safety issues at the site. The cleanup of Hanford is one of the most complex and expensive environmental remediation projects in history. The site covers 586 square miles, and the scale of the contamination is staggering. The DOE has estimated that the cleanup will take several more decades to complete and will cost hundreds of billions of dollars. The Tri-Party Agreement has provided a roadmap for the cleanup, but progress has been slow, and the project has faced numerous challenges and setbacks.

- **The Waste Treatment Plant and the Challenge of High-Level Waste:** One of the most significant components of the Hanford cleanup effort is the construction of the Waste Treatment and Immobilization Plant (WTP), also known as the vitrification plant. The WTP is designed to process the high-level radioactive waste stored in Hanford's underground tanks and convert it into glass, a process known as vitrification. The vitrified waste would then be stored in a stable form, reducing the risk of leaks and contamination. The WTP is a massive and technically complex facility, and its construction has been plagued by delays, cost overruns, and technical challenges. Originally scheduled to begin operations in 2011, the plant is now not expected to be fully operational until the 2030s. The delays have been caused by a variety of factors, including design flaws, concerns about the safety of the plant, and changes in the scope of the project. The challenge of vitrifying Hanford's high-level waste is immense, as the waste is a highly radioactive and chemically complex mixture. The DOE has had to overcome numerous technical hurdles to ensure that the vitrification process is safe and effective, and the project remains one of the most difficult aspects of the Hanford cleanup.

- **Progress and Ongoing Challenges:** Despite the many challenges, there has been significant progress in the cleanup of the Hanford Site. Several of the old reactors along the Columbia River have been dismantled and the areas around them have been cleaned up and restored. The removal of contaminated soil, the stabilization of waste sites, and the treatment of groundwater have also made important strides in reducing the environmental impact of the site. However, many challenges remain. The aging infrastructure at Hanford continues to pose risks, and the long-term management of the radioactive waste will require ongoing attention. The groundwater contamination plumes are still a major concern, and the potential for further leaks from the underground tanks is an ongoing threat. The complexity of the Hanford cleanup means that it will continue to be a focus of environmental and public health efforts for many years to come. The legacy of Hanford is a reminder of the risks and challenges associated with nuclear technology, and the need for careful management and oversight to protect future generations.

The Human and Environmental Impact: A Legacy of Contamination

- **Impact on the Local Community:** The Hanford Site has had a profound impact on the local community, particularly the residents of the nearby town of Richland, which was established to house Hanford workers. The secrecy surrounding the site during its early years meant that many residents were unaware of the dangers posed by the radioactive and chemical contaminants being released into the environment. Over the years, concerns about health impacts, particularly cancer and other diseases linked to radiation exposure, have led to numerous studies and legal battles. The Columbia River, which flows past the Hanford Site, has been a source of both sustenance and concern for local communities, including Native American tribes who have lived along its banks for thousands of years. The contamination of the river and its ecosystem has threatened traditional fishing practices and cultural sites, leading to efforts to restore and protect the river's health.
- **Environmental Impact:** The environmental impact of the Hanford Site is vast and multifaceted. The contamination of the soil, groundwater, and the Columbia River has had significant ecological consequences, affecting plant and animal life in the region. The radioactive waste stored at Hanford will remain hazardous for thousands of years, requiring long-term monitoring and management. The potential for future environmental damage remains a concern,

particularly if the cleanup efforts are not fully successful or if new incidents occur. The DOE's efforts to mitigate the environmental impact of Hanford are ongoing, but the scale of the contamination makes it a daunting task.

- **The Legacy of Hanford:** The legacy of the Hanford Nuclear Site is one of both technological achievement and environmental tragedy. While Hanford played a crucial role in the development of the U.S. nuclear arsenal and helped to shape the course of the Cold War, it also left behind a legacy of contamination and safety hazards that will take generations to address. The story of Hanford is a reminder of the complexities and risks associated with nuclear technology, and the importance of transparency, oversight, and long-term planning in managing its impact. The lessons learned from Hanford are relevant not only to other nuclear sites but also to the broader challenges of managing hazardous materials and protecting the environment in the face of technological advancement.

Chapter 24: Mayak Chemical Combine Incidents

The Mayak Chemical Combine, located in the Southern Urals of Russia, is one of the most infamous nuclear facilities in the world, largely due to a series of catastrophic incidents that occurred there throughout the mid-20th century. Built in 1948 as part of the Soviet Union's top-secret project to produce weapons-grade plutonium, Mayak played a pivotal role in the Cold War arms race. However, the facility's operations were marred by poor safety protocols, leading to a number of severe nuclear accidents. These incidents not only resulted in significant environmental contamination but also exposed thousands of people to dangerous levels of radiation, creating long-lasting health effects and ecological damage that persist to this day.

The Context of Mayak's Establishment

In the aftermath of World War II, the Soviet Union was in a frantic race to catch up with the United States in the development of nuclear weapons. The Mayak Chemical Combine was established as a key facility in this effort. Situated near the closed city of Chelyabinsk-40 (later renamed Chelyabinsk-65 and now known as Ozersk), the facility was part of the Soviet Union's ambitious plan to produce plutonium for its growing arsenal of nuclear weapons. Due to the secrecy surrounding the Soviet nuclear program, little regard was given to the potential environmental and human health impacts of the plant's operations. The urgency of the Cold War-era objectives often overshadowed concerns for safety, setting the stage for several nuclear disasters.

The 1949 Radiation Release

The first of the significant incidents at Mayak occurred in 1949, just a year after the facility began operations. On August 29, 1949, the Soviet Union conducted its first successful nuclear test, codenamed "RDS-1," at the Semipalatinsk Test Site in Kazakhstan. The plutonium for this bomb was produced at Mayak, but the rapid expansion of the plant's operations led to severe oversights in waste management. In December of that year, a substantial release of radioactive materials occurred due to an accidental discharge from a containment vessel. This incident released a considerable amount of radioactivity into the surrounding environment, contaminating a large area. The extent of the release and its impact on the local population remained classified for decades.

The Kyshtym Disaster of 1957

The most notorious incident at Mayak is undoubtedly the Kyshtym disaster, which occurred on September 29, 1957. This disaster is considered the third-largest nuclear accident in history, after the Chernobyl disaster and the Fukushima Daiichi nuclear disaster. The Kyshtym disaster was caused by the explosion of a poorly maintained storage tank containing highly radioactive waste. The cooling system for the tank had failed, causing the temperature inside to rise uncontrollably. Eventually, the buildup of heat led to a chemical explosion, which released around 20 million curies of radioactivity into the atmosphere.

The explosion caused a radioactive cloud to spread over a vast area, contaminating thousands of square kilometers of land, which became known as the East-Ural Radioactive Trace (EURT). The immediate impact was devastating, with around 10,000 people evacuated from the affected areas, though many were not informed of the true reason for their evacuation. The long-term consequences included a dramatic increase in cancer rates and other radiation-related illnesses among the local population. Despite the severity of the disaster, it remained a closely guarded secret for many years, with information only coming to light in the 1970s through the efforts of dissidents and environmental activists.

Chronic Environmental Contamination

While the Kyshtym disaster is the most well-known, it was far from the only incident at Mayak. The facility's routine operations also contributed to ongoing environmental contamination. Between 1949 and 1956, liquid radioactive waste was directly discharged into the Techa River, which flows through several villages. This led to widespread contamination of the river system, affecting the drinking water and agricultural land of the local population. Residents of the Techa River basin were exposed to radiation levels many times higher than those experienced by the populations of Hiroshima and Nagasaki after the atomic bombings.

The health effects on the local population were severe and far-reaching. Many residents suffered from acute radiation sickness, and over time, there was a marked increase in the incidence of cancers, particularly leukemia, as well as genetic mutations and birth defects. The Soviet government was slow to respond, and many affected communities were not evacuated until years later. Even after evacuation, the legacy of contamination continued, as radioactive materials persisted in the environment.

The 1967 Lake Karachay Disaster

Another significant incident linked to the Mayak Chemical Combine occurred in 1967 at Lake Karachay, a small lake near the facility that was used as a dumping ground for radioactive waste. Over the years, the lake became one of the most contaminated places on Earth. In 1967, a severe drought caused the water level in Lake Karachay to drop significantly, exposing the radioactive sediments on the lakebed.

A strong windstorm then blew radioactive dust over a large area, leading to further contamination of the surrounding region.

The spread of radioactive particles from Lake Karachay added to the already high levels of environmental radiation in the area. The event further exacerbated health issues for the local population, including increased rates of cancer and other radiation-induced diseases. Lake Karachay itself remains a symbol of the environmental devastation caused by Mayak, and it is considered one of the most polluted sites on the planet. The lake's lethal levels of radiation are so intense that spending even a short amount of time near its shores can result in a fatal dose of radiation.

Legacy and Long-Term Consequences

The Mayak Chemical Combine incidents collectively represent some of the most significant nuclear tragedies in history. The environmental and human toll of these disasters is immense, with the full extent of the damage only becoming apparent decades later. The secrecy surrounding the Soviet nuclear program meant that many of the affected communities were left in the dark about the dangers they faced, and it wasn't until years later that the true scale of the contamination was revealed.

In the years since, efforts have been made to remediate the most contaminated areas, but the legacy of Mayak remains. The site itself continues to be a focus of concern, as it still houses significant amounts of radioactive waste. Moreover, the health effects on the local population continue to be studied, with many residents suffering from the long-term consequences of radiation exposure. The Mayak incidents serve as a stark reminder of the dangers of nuclear technology when safety is compromised, and they highlight the need for transparency and accountability in managing nuclear materials.

Chapter 25: Mordechai Vanunu Disclosure

Mordechai Vanunu, an Israeli former nuclear technician, is one of the most significant whistleblowers in modern history. His actions and subsequent revelations fundamentally altered global perceptions of Israel's nuclear capabilities. Born in 1954 in Marrakesh, Morocco, Vanunu immigrated to Israel with his family in 1963. He later studied at Ben-Gurion University of the Negev, where he became increasingly disillusioned with the Israeli government and its policies, particularly regarding its secretive nuclear program. Vanunu's eventual disclosure in 1986 of Israel's nuclear weapons program to the British press exposed one of the most closely guarded secrets of the Israeli state, leading to his abduction by Mossad, imprisonment, and international notoriety.

The Development of Israel's Nuclear Program

Israel's nuclear program began in the 1950s, motivated by a desire to secure a strategic deterrent against hostile neighboring states. With assistance from France, Israel constructed the Dimona nuclear reactor in the Negev Desert. Officially described as a textile plant and later as a facility for peaceful nuclear research, the reactor was, in fact, central to Israel's clandestine efforts to develop nuclear weapons. The Israeli government maintained a policy of deliberate ambiguity regarding its nuclear capabilities, neither confirming nor denying the possession of nuclear weapons. This ambiguity allowed Israel to avoid direct confrontation over its nuclear activities while deterring potential adversaries.

Over the decades, the Dimona facility became the heart of Israel's nuclear weapons production. The country's leaders believed that maintaining secrecy around its nuclear capabilities was essential for national security, ensuring that Israel would never be pressured into nuclear disarmament by the international community. By the 1980s, Israel was widely believed to have developed a significant stockpile of nuclear weapons, though the details remained speculative and unconfirmed until Vanunu's disclosures.

Mordechai Vanunu's Employment at Dimona

In 1976, Mordechai Vanunu was employed as a technician at the Negev Nuclear Research Center in Dimona. Over the next nine years, Vanunu worked in various capacities within the facility, gaining access to sensitive information about the inner workings of Israel's nuclear program. During his time at Dimona, Vanunu grew increasingly critical of Israel's policies and the secrecy surrounding its nuclear activities. His disillusionment was fueled by both political and moral considerations, particularly his opposition to Israel's treatment of Palestinians and his belief that the world had a right to know about the country's nuclear arsenal.

In 1985, after a series of disagreements with his superiors and amid growing dissatisfaction, Vanunu was laid off from his position at Dimona. He subsequently traveled to various countries, eventually converting to Christianity and renouncing his Israeli citizenship. During his travels, Vanunu made contact with journalists and began considering the possibility of revealing what he knew about Israel's nuclear program.

The Disclosure: Vanunu's Revelations to the Sunday Times

In 1986, Mordechai Vanunu approached the British press with his story, eventually securing a meeting with reporters from The Sunday Times. Over several sessions, Vanunu provided detailed information about the Dimona facility, including photographs he had secretly taken while employed there. His revelations were groundbreaking, offering the first concrete evidence that Israel had developed a substantial arsenal of nuclear weapons. Vanunu estimated that Israel possessed between 100 and 200 nuclear warheads, a figure far higher than most analysts had previously suspected.

The Sunday Times conducted extensive research to verify Vanunu's claims, consulting with nuclear experts who confirmed the authenticity of the information he provided. On October 5, 1986, The Sunday Times published an extensive exposé titled "Inside Dimona: Israel's Nuclear Bomb Factory," which detailed the scope of Israel's nuclear weapons program based on Vanunu's disclosures. The article sent shockwaves through the international community, challenging the Israeli government's policy of ambiguity and raising new concerns about nuclear proliferation in the Middle East.

The Mossad Operation: Vanunu's Abduction

The Israeli government, upon learning of Vanunu's intentions and subsequent disclosures, acted swiftly to neutralize what they perceived as a grave threat to national security. The Mossad, Israel's intelligence agency, launched a covert operation to capture Vanunu and bring him back to Israel. Posing as an American tourist, a female Mossad agent lured Vanunu from London to Rome under the pretense of a romantic relationship. Once in Rome, Vanunu was drugged, abducted, and smuggled back to Israel on a cargo ship.

Vanunu's kidnapping in Rome was a clear violation of international law, sparking outrage and condemnation from various human rights organizations and governments. However, the Israeli government justified its actions on the grounds of national security, arguing that Vanunu had betrayed his country by revealing classified information.

The Trial and Imprisonment

Upon his return to Israel, Mordechai Vanunu was charged with treason and espionage. His trial was conducted in secret, with the Israeli government imposing strict censorship on media coverage of the proceedings. In 1988, Vanunu was convicted and sentenced to 18 years in prison, 11 of which were spent in solitary confinement. The harsh conditions of his imprisonment, including extended periods of isolation, were widely criticized by human rights organizations, which argued that they constituted cruel and inhumane treatment.

During his time in prison, Vanunu continued to assert that his actions were motivated by a desire to prevent nuclear proliferation and to promote transparency. He viewed himself as a whistleblower who had acted in the public interest, rather than as a traitor. Despite the severe restrictions placed on him, Vanunu managed to smuggle out letters and statements, which were published by his supporters and attracted international attention.

International Reactions and the Impact of Vanunu's Disclosure

Mordechai Vanunu's disclosure had a profound impact on global perceptions of Israel's nuclear program. While it was widely believed that Israel possessed nuclear weapons, Vanunu's revelations provided the first concrete evidence of the scale and sophistication of the program. The disclosure intensified debates over nuclear proliferation in the Middle East, with many countries calling for greater transparency and for Israel to sign the Nuclear Non-Proliferation Treaty (NPT).

However, the Israeli government maintained its policy of nuclear ambiguity, neither confirming nor denying the existence of its nuclear arsenal. This stance allowed Israel to avoid the international scrutiny and pressure that might have come with an open acknowledgment of its nuclear capabilities. At the same time, Vanunu's disclosure heightened tensions in the region, as neighboring countries expressed concerns about Israel's nuclear deterrent and the potential for a nuclear arms race in the Middle East.

International reactions to Vanunu's imprisonment were mixed. While some governments and organizations called for his release on humanitarian grounds, others supported Israel's actions, citing the sensitive nature of the information he had disclosed. Human rights organizations, including Amnesty International, campaigned for Vanunu's release, arguing that his prolonged solitary confinement constituted a violation of his basic rights. Despite these efforts, Vanunu remained in prison until 2004, serving the full 18-year sentence.

Release and Continued Restrictions

Mordechai Vanunu was released from prison on April 21, 2004, after serving his full sentence. However, his release came with stringent conditions, including restrictions on his movement, communication, and association. He was prohibited from leaving Israel, speaking to foreign journalists, or accessing the internet. These restrictions were justified by the Israeli government on the grounds that Vanunu still possessed classified information that could harm national security if disclosed.

Vanunu repeatedly challenged these restrictions, arguing that they violated his fundamental rights to freedom of expression and movement. He expressed a desire to leave Israel and start a new life abroad, but his requests to do so were consistently denied by the Israeli authorities. Over the years, Vanunu was arrested several times for violating the terms of his release, including for giving interviews to foreign media outlets.

Legacy and Ongoing Controversy

Mordechai Vanunu's legacy remains a subject of intense debate. To his supporters, he is a hero who took great personal risks to expose a secret that he believed posed a danger to global security. They argue that Vanunu's actions were motivated by a commitment to peace and transparency and that his treatment by the Israeli government has been unjust and disproportionate.

To his detractors, Vanunu is a traitor who betrayed his country and endangered its security by revealing sensitive information to foreign governments. They contend that his actions justified the severe response from the Israeli government, including his prolonged imprisonment and the ongoing restrictions on his freedom.

The broader implications of Vanunu's disclosure continue to resonate in discussions about nuclear proliferation, whistleblowing, and the balance between national security and individual rights. His case has been cited in debates over the protection of whistleblowers, with some arguing that Vanunu's treatment has had a chilling effect on others who might consider exposing government wrongdoing.

Chapter 26: Church Rock Uranium Mill Spill

The Church Rock Uranium Mill Spill is one of the most significant yet often overlooked environmental disasters in United States history. Occurring on July 16, 1979, near the small community of Church Rock in northwestern New Mexico, this catastrophic event released vast quantities of radioactive waste into the environment, profoundly impacting the land, water, and people of the Navajo Nation. The spill stands as the largest release of radioactive material in the United States, surpassing even the Three Mile Island nuclear accident in terms of the sheer volume of radioactive contaminants released. However, despite its scale and the severe consequences, the Church Rock spill received far less attention and remains relatively unknown to the broader public.

The Context: Uranium Mining on Navajo Land

To understand the Church Rock Uranium Mill Spill, it is essential to grasp the broader context of uranium mining on Navajo land. In the mid-20th century, during the height of the Cold War, the United States government sought to secure a steady supply of uranium to fuel its burgeoning nuclear weapons program. The American Southwest, particularly the Colorado Plateau, became a focal point for uranium mining due to its rich deposits of the radioactive mineral. Large areas of the Navajo Nation, which spans parts of Arizona, Utah, and New Mexico, were identified as prime sites for mining operations.

For the Navajo people, the arrival of uranium mining presented a complex set of challenges and opportunities. On one hand, the industry promised economic development and jobs in an impoverished region. On the other hand, it introduced significant environmental and health risks that were not fully understood or communicated to the local population. Many Navajo workers were employed in the mines, often without adequate protection or information about the dangers of radiation exposure. Over time, the consequences of uranium mining became painfully apparent, with increased rates of cancer, respiratory illnesses, and environmental degradation throughout the Navajo Nation.

The United Nuclear Corporation (UNC) Mill

The site of the Church Rock spill was a uranium mill owned and operated by the United Nuclear Corporation (UNC). The mill processed uranium ore extracted from nearby mines, using a series of chemical processes to separate the valuable uranium from the surrounding rock. The resulting uranium concentrate, often referred to as "yellowcake," was then used as raw material for nuclear fuel or weapons. The waste byproducts of this process, known as tailings, were highly radioactive and contained a variety of hazardous chemicals.

To manage these tailings, UNC constructed a large, unlined tailings pond near the mill site. The pond was designed to hold the liquid and solid waste materials, allowing the radioactive particles to settle to the bottom while the water evaporated. However, the design and construction of the pond were inadequate for the volume of waste being produced, and concerns about its stability were raised by some employees and local residents. Despite these concerns, operations continued, and the tailings pond grew larger as more waste was deposited.

The Spill: July 16, 1979

In the early hours of July 16, 1979, the dam containing the tailings pond at the UNC mill site failed, releasing approximately 1,100 tons of solid radioactive mill waste and 94 million gallons of acidic, radioactive wastewater into the Puerco River. The breach was caused by a combination of factors, including structural weaknesses in the dam, the buildup of pressure from the large volume of waste, and the failure to adequately monitor and maintain the facility. The resulting spill was a disaster of unprecedented scale, with radioactive contaminants quickly spreading downstream.

The Puerco River, a normally dry riverbed that only flowed during periods of heavy rain, became a conduit for the toxic waste, carrying it through the arid landscape and into the Navajo Nation. The contaminated water flowed for more than 80 miles, crossing into Arizona and affecting numerous communities along its path. The immediate impact was devastating, as the radioactive water contaminated drinking wells, irrigation systems, and grazing lands, threatening the health and livelihoods of thousands of Navajo people.

Immediate Response and Initial Impact

The initial response to the Church Rock spill was slow and inadequate, reflecting a broader pattern of neglect and environmental injustice faced by Indigenous communities in the United States. Local residents were not immediately informed of the dangers posed by the spill, and many continued to use the contaminated water for drinking, cooking, and agriculture. The Navajo people, who had long relied on the Puerco River for their daily needs, were left vulnerable to the toxic exposure.

UNC and government agencies, including the Environmental Protection Agency (EPA) and the Nuclear Regulatory Commission (NRC), were slow to respond to the disaster. Although cleanup efforts eventually began, they were limited in scope and effectiveness. Much of the radioactive waste remained in the environment, and the contaminated areas were never fully restored. The spill's impact on the land and water resources of the Navajo Nation was profound and long-lasting, with many of the effects persisting for decades.

Health and Environmental Consequences

The health consequences of the Church Rock spill were severe and far-reaching. The radioactive contaminants released into the environment included uranium, thorium, radium, and other toxic substances, all of which pose significant risks to human health. Prolonged exposure to these materials can lead to a range of illnesses, including cancer, kidney disease, and respiratory problems. For the Navajo people, who were already disproportionately affected by the health impacts of uranium mining, the spill exacerbated existing health disparities.

One of the most insidious effects of the spill was the contamination of drinking water sources. Many Navajo families relied on wells and natural springs for their water, and the radioactive waste from the spill infiltrated these sources, rendering them unsafe. Even after the spill, many residents continued to use contaminated water, unaware of the risks. This prolonged exposure to radiation likely contributed to increased rates of cancer and other illnesses in the affected communities.

The environmental impact of the spill was equally devastating. The Puerco River, once a vital resource for the Navajo people, became a source of toxic pollution. The radioactive contaminants settled into the riverbed and surrounding soils, creating a long-term environmental hazard. Livestock that grazed on contaminated land or drank from the river were exposed to radiation, further spreading the contamination through the food chain. The spill also disrupted traditional agricultural practices, as the contaminated land became unsuitable for farming.

Legal and Regulatory Aftermath

The Church Rock Uranium Mill Spill highlighted significant shortcomings in the regulation and oversight of the uranium mining industry. The failure of the dam and the subsequent spill were the result of a combination of factors, including inadequate design, poor maintenance, and insufficient regulatory scrutiny. In the aftermath of the disaster, there were calls for greater oversight and stricter regulations to prevent similar incidents in the future.

The legal response to the spill was complicated and protracted. The Navajo Nation, along with affected residents, sought compensation and accountability from UNC and the federal government. However, legal battles were drawn out over many years, with many of the claims ultimately being dismissed or settled for amounts that did not fully compensate for the damage done. The spill also prompted a reevaluation of the environmental regulations governing uranium milling and mining, but meaningful reforms were slow to materialize.

The Church Rock spill also brought attention to the broader issue of environmental justice. The disaster highlighted the disproportionate impact of environmental hazards on Indigenous communities and the failure of government agencies to protect vulnerable populations. In the years that followed, the Navajo Nation and other Indigenous groups became increasingly vocal in advocating for their rights and demanding greater protection from environmental harm.

Long-Term Consequences and Ongoing Struggles

The legacy of the Church Rock Uranium Mill Spill continues to affect the Navajo Nation to this day. Despite some cleanup efforts, much of the contamination remains in the environment, posing ongoing risks to human health and the ecosystem. The spill is part of a broader pattern of environmental degradation and neglect that has plagued the Navajo Nation for decades, largely as a result of the uranium mining industry.

For many Navajo people, the spill has had lasting psychological and cultural impacts as well. The loss of access to clean water and land has disrupted traditional ways of life, and the ongoing threat of radiation exposure has created a pervasive sense of fear and uncertainty. The spill also deepened mistrust between the Navajo Nation and the federal government, as many residents felt that their concerns were ignored or dismissed.

Efforts to address the long-term consequences of the spill have been hampered by a lack of resources and political will. Although there have been some attempts to clean up the contamination and provide compensation to affected residents, these efforts have often fallen short. Many of the affected communities continue to struggle with the health and environmental impacts of the spill, and the broader issue of uranium contamination on Navajo land remains unresolved.

Recognition and Awareness

One of the most significant challenges in addressing the legacy of the Church Rock spill is the lack of public awareness. Despite being the largest release of radioactive material in U.S. history, the spill has received relatively little attention compared to other nuclear disasters, such as Three Mile Island or Chernobyl. This lack of recognition has made it difficult to generate the political and public support needed to address the ongoing impacts of the disaster.

In recent years, there has been a growing movement to raise awareness about the Church Rock spill and its consequences. Indigenous activists, environmental organizations, and scholars have worked to document the history of the spill and advocate for greater accountability and reparations. These efforts have helped to bring attention to the environmental injustices faced by the Navajo Nation and have sparked broader discussions about the legacy of uranium mining in the American Southwest.

Chapter 27: INEL Spent Fuel Handling Incident

The INEL (Idaho National Engineering Laboratory) Spent Fuel Handling Incident, which occurred in January 1961, is a lesser-known yet critical event in the history of nuclear energy. Located in southeastern Idaho, INEL, now known as the Idaho National Laboratory (INL), was a key site for nuclear research and development during the mid-20th century. The incident involved a catastrophic explosion at the Stationary Low-Power Reactor Number One (SL-1), resulting in the deaths of three military personnel and highlighting the severe risks associated with nuclear reactor operations, especially during the early years of nuclear power development. This incident serves as a grim reminder of the potential dangers inherent in nuclear technology, particularly in handling spent nuclear fuel and reactor maintenance.

Background: The Idaho National Engineering Laboratory

INEL was established in 1949 as part of the United States Atomic Energy Commission (AEC), with the goal of advancing nuclear technology for both civilian and military applications. The laboratory played a central role in the development of various nuclear reactors, including those used for power generation, research, and military purposes. The remote location of INEL in the high desert of Idaho was chosen to minimize the risks to populated areas in the event of an accident.

One of the projects undertaken at INEL was the development of the Stationary Low-Power Reactor Number One (SL-1). The SL-1 was a small, experimental reactor designed to provide electrical power and heating for remote military installations, such as radar stations in the Arctic. The reactor was part of the Army's Nuclear Power Program, which sought to develop portable and easily deployable nuclear reactors that could operate in isolated locations. The SL-1 reactor was intended to demonstrate the feasibility of this concept, with the potential for deployment in harsh environments where conventional power sources were unavailable.

The Design and Operation of the SL-1 Reactor

The SL-1 reactor was a prototype of a simple, compact, and transportable reactor design. It used highly enriched uranium fuel and operated at a relatively low power output of 3 megawatts thermal (MWt). The reactor's design was based on the boiling water reactor (BWR) concept, where water served as both the coolant and the moderator, and steam generated from the boiling water was used to drive a turbine for electricity generation.

The reactor core consisted of 40 fuel assemblies arranged in a cylindrical configuration, with control rods inserted from the top to regulate the nuclear reaction. The control rods, made of boron carbide, were used to absorb neutrons and control the rate of fission within the reactor. The SL-1 reactor was designed to be manually operated, with the control rods being raised and lowered by hand to start up or shut down the reactor.

While the SL-1 reactor was an innovative design, it also had several inherent risks, particularly due to its manual control system. The reactor's compact size and the high reactivity of its fuel made it susceptible to rapid changes in power output, which could lead to dangerous conditions if not properly managed. Moreover, the reactor's design placed significant responsibility on the operators to ensure safe operation, with little margin for error.

The Incident: January 3, 1961

On January 3, 1961, a tragic accident occurred during a routine maintenance procedure at the SL-1 reactor. The incident involved three U.S. Army personnel: Army Specialist Richard Leroy McKinley, Army Specialist John A. Byrnes, and Navy Electrician's Mate Richard C. Legg. The men were tasked with performing maintenance on the reactor, including the reinstallation of a control rod that had been removed for servicing.

As part of the maintenance procedure, the control rod needed to be manually lifted and reinserted into the reactor core. However, during this operation, the control rod was inadvertently withdrawn too far, leading to a criticality accident. When the control rod was pulled out beyond a certain point, it caused a sudden and uncontrolled increase in the reactor's power output, known as a "prompt critical" event. This rapid rise in power caused the reactor core to overheat almost instantaneously, resulting in a steam explosion.

The explosion was devastating, causing severe damage to the reactor and the surrounding building. The force of the blast was so powerful that it ruptured the reactor vessel, releasing a significant amount of radioactive material into the environment. The three men working on the reactor were killed instantly, with their bodies being subjected to extreme radiation exposure and physical trauma. The blast was so intense that one of the men, Richard C. Legg, was impaled on the ceiling of the reactor building by a control rod that had been ejected from the core.

Immediate Aftermath and Response

The explosion at the SL-1 reactor was quickly detected by radiation monitors and alarms, prompting an immediate response from INEL personnel. Emergency crews were dispatched to the site, but they faced significant challenges due to the high levels of radiation in the reactor building. The extent of the radiation contamination made it difficult for rescuers to enter the building and recover the bodies of the deceased men.

The incident was a major crisis for INEL and the Army Nuclear Power Program. The explosion not only resulted in the loss of life but also raised serious concerns about the safety of the SL-1 reactor design and the procedures used for handling spent fuel and reactor maintenance. The AEC, along with other federal agencies, launched a thorough investigation to determine the cause of the accident and to assess the broader implications for nuclear reactor safety.

The Investigation: Causes and Findings

The investigation into the SL-1 incident was one of the most detailed and comprehensive inquiries into a nuclear accident up to that time. The AEC, along with experts from the National Reactor Testing Station (NRTS) and other agencies, conducted an extensive analysis of the reactor's design, the events leading up to the explosion, and the actions of the personnel involved.

The investigation revealed that the root cause of the accident was the rapid withdrawal of the control rod, which led to the reactor becoming prompt critical. The exact reason why the control rod was withdrawn too far remains uncertain, but several theories were proposed. One theory suggested that the rod may have been stuck or difficult to move, requiring additional force to be applied, which could have led to it being pulled out too quickly. Another theory posited that the men may have been unaware of the precise position of the control rod due to poor visibility or confusion during the maintenance procedure.

The investigation also highlighted several design flaws in the SL-1 reactor, including the lack of automated safety systems to prevent the withdrawal of the control rods beyond a safe limit. The manual operation of the reactor placed a significant burden on the operators, increasing the risk of human error. The investigation concluded that the incident was primarily the result of a combination of human error and design deficiencies.

Environmental and Health Impact

The SL-1 explosion had significant environmental and health consequences. The release of radioactive material from the reactor contaminated the surrounding area, including the air, soil, and water. The most immediate concern was the exposure of the emergency response teams to high levels of radiation, as they worked to secure the site and recover the bodies of the victims. Despite the protective gear used by the responders, some individuals received substantial radiation doses, although no immediate fatalities resulted from this exposure.

The environmental contamination from the SL-1 incident required extensive cleanup efforts. The reactor building was decontaminated, and the surrounding area was monitored for radiation levels. The reactor core and other radioactive materials were eventually removed from the site and buried in a secure disposal facility. The cleanup process took several years to complete, and the site remained a point of concern for environmental monitoring for decades.

In addition to the environmental impact, the incident also had lasting health implications for those involved in the response and cleanup efforts. The high levels of radiation exposure posed significant risks for the development of long-term health effects, including cancer and other radiation-related illnesses. The incident served as a stark reminder of the dangers posed by nuclear accidents, not only to those directly involved but also to the broader community and environment.

Lessons Learned and Impact on Nuclear Safety

The INEL Spent Fuel Handling Incident had a profound impact on the nuclear industry, particularly in the areas of reactor design, safety procedures, and spent fuel handling. The incident underscored the critical importance of safety in nuclear operations, leading to several key lessons and changes in the industry.

One of the most significant lessons from the SL-1 incident was the need for more robust and automated safety systems in nuclear reactors. The manual operation of the SL-1 reactor, combined with the lack of fail-safes to prevent the withdrawal of the control rods beyond a certain point, was identified as a major design flaw. In response, future reactor designs incorporated more automated controls and safety features to reduce the reliance on human operators and to prevent similar accidents from occurring.

The incident also highlighted the importance of thorough training and procedural safeguards for personnel involved in nuclear operations. The complexity of nuclear reactor systems and the potential consequences of errors necessitate rigorous training and clear, standardized procedures for maintenance and operations. The SL-1 accident led to a renewed focus on operator training, with an emphasis on understanding the risks associated with reactor maintenance and spent fuel handling.

Furthermore, the incident contributed to the development of more stringent regulations and oversight for the nuclear industry. The AEC and other regulatory bodies implemented new safety standards and inspection protocols to ensure that nuclear facilities operated with the highest levels of safety and security. The lessons learned from the SL-1 incident informed broader efforts to improve nuclear safety across the industry, influencing both civilian and military nuclear programs.

Public Perception and Legacy

The SL-1 incident had a lasting impact on public perception of nuclear energy and the risks associated with it. Although the incident did not receive the same level of public attention as later nuclear accidents, such as the Three Mile Island or Chernobyl disasters, it nonetheless contributed to growing concerns about the safety of nuclear power. The incident served as an early warning of the potential dangers of nuclear technology, particularly when safety measures are inadequate or when human error is a factor.

In the years following the SL-1 incident, the nuclear industry faced increasing scrutiny and opposition from the public and environmental groups. The incident became part of the broader narrative of nuclear accidents and mishaps that fueled debates about the viability and safety of nuclear power. While the nuclear industry continued to advance, the SL-1 incident remained a sobering reminder of the need for constant vigilance and commitment to safety.

Chapter 28: Soviet Submarine K-431 Reactor Accident

The Soviet Submarine K-431 Reactor Accident stands as one of the most harrowing nuclear incidents in naval history. On August 10, 1985, a catastrophic explosion occurred aboard the Soviet Echo-class submarine K-431, formerly known as K-31, while it was docked at the Chazhma Bay naval base near Vladivostok in the Russian Far East. This incident, involving the submarine's nuclear reactor, resulted in the deaths of ten crew members and the release of a significant amount of radioactive material into the environment. The K-431 reactor accident serves as a stark reminder of the dangers associated with nuclear-powered submarines and the profound consequences of mishandling nuclear materials.

Background: The Soviet Echo-Class Submarine Program

The K-431 was part of the Soviet Navy's Echo-class of nuclear-powered submarines, which were developed during the Cold War era. The Echo-class submarines, known in Russia as Project 675, were primarily designed for anti-ship warfare and were equipped with nuclear-tipped cruise missiles. These submarines were among the Soviet Union's first nuclear-powered submarines and played a crucial role in the Soviet Navy's strategy of deterrence and power projection during the Cold War.

The Echo-class submarines were powered by two pressurized water reactors (PWRs), which provided the necessary energy for propulsion and onboard systems. The use of nuclear reactors allowed these submarines to operate for extended periods without the need for refueling, giving them a significant strategic advantage. However, the complexity of nuclear reactors also introduced substantial risks, particularly during maintenance and refueling operations.

The K-431, originally commissioned as K-31 in 1965, had undergone several years of service before it was renamed and assigned to the Pacific Fleet. By the mid-1980s, the submarine was due for a routine refueling operation, during which the reactor cores would be replaced with fresh nuclear fuel. This operation was to take place at the Chazhma Bay naval base, a major facility for the maintenance and repair of the Soviet Navy's Pacific Fleet submarines.

The Refueling Operation: A Critical and Dangerous Task

Refueling a nuclear-powered submarine is a complex and inherently dangerous task that requires meticulous planning, precision, and adherence to strict safety protocols. The process involves the removal of spent nuclear fuel from the reactor core and the installation of fresh fuel assemblies. During this operation, the reactor must be carefully controlled to prevent any accidental criticality events—situations in which the nuclear fission reaction becomes self-sustaining and uncontrollable.

On the day of the accident, the K-431 was undergoing a routine refueling operation. The reactor compartment had been opened, and the spent fuel was being removed from the reactor core. The operation was overseen by a team of naval personnel and engineers who were responsible for ensuring that the reactor remained in a safe and stable condition throughout the process.

However, during the refueling operation, a critical error occurred. The reactor's control rod assembly—a crucial component used to regulate the fission reaction—was mistakenly raised too far, leading to an accidental reactivity excursion. This action caused the reactor to go prompt critical, resulting in an uncontrolled increase in the power output of the reactor.

The Explosion: A Catastrophic Event

The prompt criticality of the reactor led to a catastrophic steam explosion within the reactor compartment. The rapid increase in temperature and pressure caused the reactor vessel to rupture, releasing a massive amount of energy in the form of heat and radiation. The explosion was so powerful that it blew off the submarine's reactor compartment cover, sending it flying into the air and landing several meters away from the submarine.

The explosion immediately killed ten naval personnel who were in or near the reactor compartment at the time. The intense heat and radiation released by the explosion also caused severe injuries to several other crew members and workers on the submarine. The blast was so violent that it caused significant structural damage to the submarine, as well as to the dock and surrounding facilities at the Chazhma Bay naval base.

In addition to the immediate human casualties, the explosion released a large amount of radioactive material into the environment. The radioactive cloud spread over the naval base and the surrounding area, contaminating the air, soil, and water. The release of radioactivity posed a serious health risk to the naval personnel, workers, and residents in the vicinity of the base.

Emergency Response and Containment Efforts

The explosion aboard the K-431 triggered an immediate emergency response from the Soviet Navy and other military and civilian authorities. Firefighters, medical teams, and radiation specialists were quickly dispatched to the scene to contain the fire, treat the injured, and assess the extent of the radioactive contamination.

One of the primary concerns was the potential for further explosions or leaks of radioactive material from the damaged reactor. The reactor core, now exposed to the open air, continued to emit radiation, posing a serious threat to the safety of the emergency response teams. Despite the risks, the response teams worked tirelessly to contain the situation, extinguish the fires, and secure the reactor compartment.

The contaminated areas of the naval base were cordoned off, and decontamination efforts were initiated to reduce the spread of radioactive material. Specialized equipment was brought in to monitor radiation levels and to identify the most heavily contaminated areas. The reactor core was eventually stabilized, and the remaining nuclear fuel was removed from the submarine under strict safety protocols.

The response to the K-431 incident required the mobilization of significant resources and personnel, including military and civilian experts in nuclear safety. Despite the successful containment of the immediate danger, the incident had long-lasting effects on the health and safety of those involved in the response efforts, as well as on the broader environment.

Health and Environmental Impact

The K-431 reactor accident had severe health consequences for the naval personnel, workers, and emergency responders who were exposed to the explosion and the subsequent radioactive contamination. The ten men who were killed in the explosion died instantly from a combination of physical trauma, burns, and acute radiation exposure. Several other individuals who were exposed to high levels of radiation during the initial explosion and the subsequent containment efforts suffered from acute radiation sickness (ARS), a condition characterized by nausea, vomiting, fatigue, and, in severe cases, death.

The long-term health effects of the incident were also significant. Many of those who were involved in the response and cleanup operations experienced long-term health problems, including an increased risk of cancer and other radiation-related illnesses. The psychological impact of the incident on survivors and their families was profound, as they grappled with the trauma of the event and the long-term uncertainty surrounding their health.

The environmental impact of the K-431 accident was also severe. The release of radioactive material into the air, soil, and water at the Chazhma Bay naval base led to widespread contamination. The surrounding area, including the nearby village of Shkotovo-22 (now known as Bolshoy Kamen), was exposed to elevated levels of radiation. The contamination affected the local ecosystem, including marine life in the bay, and posed a long-term environmental hazard.

Decontamination efforts were extensive and costly, involving the removal of contaminated soil, the cleaning of buildings and equipment, and the monitoring of radiation levels in the environment. Despite these efforts, some areas remained contaminated for years, and the full extent of the environmental damage caused by the incident is difficult to quantify.

The Soviet Response: Secrecy and Censorship

In typical Cold War fashion, the Soviet government initially responded to the K-431 reactor accident with a high level of secrecy and censorship. The Soviet Union had a long-standing policy of downplaying or concealing nuclear accidents, both to protect its image internationally and to prevent public panic domestically. As a result, information about the K-431 incident was tightly controlled, and details about the explosion and its aftermath were not made public for several years.

The official Soviet narrative minimized the severity of the accident, with initial reports framing the incident as a minor explosion with limited consequences. The full extent of the radioactive contamination, the health impacts on the personnel involved, and the environmental damage were not disclosed to the public. Families of the victims were provided with limited information, and many were left in the dark about the true cause of the deaths of their loved ones.

It was not until years later, following the collapse of the Soviet Union and the subsequent opening of government archives, that more detailed information about the K-431 reactor accident became available. The declassification of documents and testimonies from survivors provided a fuller picture of the events leading up to the explosion, the response efforts, and the long-term consequences of the incident.

Lessons Learned and Impact on Nuclear Safety

The K-431 reactor accident had a significant impact on the Soviet Navy's approach to nuclear safety and reactor operations. The incident highlighted the critical importance of strict adherence to safety protocols during the refueling and maintenance of nuclear reactors. The accidental reactivity excursion that led to the explosion was a direct result of human error and procedural lapses, underscoring the need for more rigorous training and oversight of personnel involved in nuclear operations.

In the aftermath of the accident, the Soviet Navy conducted a thorough review of its nuclear safety practices and implemented several key changes. These changes included improved safety protocols for reactor refueling, enhanced training for reactor operators, and the development of more advanced safety systems to prevent accidental criticality events. The incident also led to a reevaluation of the design and construction of nuclear-powered submarines, with an emphasis on reducing the risks associated with reactor operations.

The K-431 incident also contributed to broader efforts within the Soviet Union to improve transparency and accountability in the handling of nuclear materials. The secrecy surrounding the incident, combined with the growing international scrutiny of the Soviet Union's nuclear program, led to increased pressure for more open reporting and oversight of nuclear accidents. While the Soviet government continued to maintain a high level of secrecy around its nuclear activities, the K-431 accident marked a turning point in the recognition of the need for greater transparency and safety in the nuclear industry.

Chapter 29: Los Alamos Criticality Accident

The Los Alamos Criticality Accident of 1958 is one of the most significant and tragic incidents in the history of nuclear research in the United States. This accident, which took place at the Los Alamos Scientific Laboratory in New Mexico, resulted in the death of one scientist and the severe radiation exposure of several others. The incident occurred during the handling of plutonium, a highly radioactive material used in nuclear weapons, and highlighted the inherent dangers of working with fissile materials in a research environment. The Los Alamos Criticality Accident is a stark reminder of the risks associated with nuclear research and the importance of rigorous safety protocols to prevent such incidents.

Background: The Los Alamos Scientific Laboratory

The Los Alamos Scientific Laboratory (LASL), now known as Los Alamos National Laboratory (LANL), was established during World War II as part of the Manhattan Project, the United States' secret effort to develop atomic weapons. Located in the remote high desert of northern New Mexico, Los Alamos became the epicenter of nuclear research, attracting some of the most brilliant scientific minds of the time, including J. Robert Oppenheimer, Enrico Fermi, and Richard Feynman. The laboratory played a crucial role in the development of the first atomic bombs, which were used in the bombings of Hiroshima and Nagasaki in 1945.

In the years following World War II, Los Alamos continued to be a hub for nuclear research, focusing on the development and refinement of nuclear weapons, as well as research into nuclear reactors and other applications of nuclear energy. The laboratory's work involved the handling and experimentation with fissile materials, such as uranium and plutonium, which are capable of sustaining nuclear fission reactions. The research conducted at Los Alamos was essential to the United States' nuclear arsenal and its position as a superpower during the Cold War.

However, the work at Los Alamos was not without its risks. The handling of fissile materials is an inherently dangerous task, as these materials can become critical—meaning they can sustain a nuclear chain reaction—if not handled with extreme care. A criticality accident occurs when a fissile material assembly becomes supercritical, leading to an uncontrolled release of energy in the form of radiation. Such accidents can be deadly, as they expose workers to lethal doses of radiation in a matter of seconds.

The Incident: A Routine Experiment Gone Wrong

On December 30, 1958, a routine experiment was being conducted at the Los Alamos Scientific Laboratory's Technical Area 18 (TA-18), also known as the "Criticality Experiment Facility." This facility was specifically designed for conducting experiments with fissile materials to better understand the conditions under which a nuclear chain reaction could occur. The experiments involved carefully arranging plutonium or enriched uranium in different configurations to measure their criticality—the point at which a self-sustaining nuclear chain reaction would begin.

On the day of the accident, a team of scientists and technicians, led by a highly experienced scientist named Cecil Kelley, was working on an experiment involving a large cylindrical mixing tank containing an aqueous solution of plutonium nitrate. The solution was being used to study the properties of plutonium under various chemical and physical conditions. Kelley, a 40-year-old chemical operator with over a decade of experience at Los Alamos, was responsible for operating the mixing tank and ensuring that the plutonium solution remained in a safe, subcritical state.

However, during the course of the experiment, a critical error occurred. The exact sequence of events leading to the accident remains a subject of some debate, but it is generally believed that an unexpected increase in the concentration of plutonium in the tank caused the solution to reach a critical state. This sudden criticality resulted in a burst of neutron radiation and gamma rays, which were emitted from the tank in a matter of milliseconds.

The Explosion of Radiation: A Fatal Dose

When the plutonium solution in the mixing tank went critical, it produced a massive and instantaneous release of radiation. The burst of neutron radiation, which lasted for only a fraction of a second, was accompanied by intense gamma radiation. The total energy released was relatively small in terms of explosive power—equivalent to only a few kilograms of TNT—but the radiation dose was lethal to anyone in close proximity to the tank.

Cecil Kelley, who was standing near the tank at the time of the accident, received the brunt of the radiation exposure. The radiation dose he received was estimated to be around 12,000 to 20,000 rem (Roentgen Equivalent Man), a dose far exceeding the lethal threshold. For comparison, a dose of around 450 rem is considered lethal to 50% of people exposed without medical treatment. Kelley was instantly incapacitated by the radiation burst, experiencing severe nausea, dizziness, and confusion.

Despite his critical condition, Kelley was able to stagger out of the room and call for help before collapsing. His colleagues, who were working nearby, quickly realized that a criticality accident had occurred and immediately evacuated the area. Emergency response teams were called to the scene, and Kelley was rushed to the Los Alamos Medical Center, where doctors worked frantically to treat his injuries.

The Aftermath: Cecil Kelley's Struggle for Life

Cecil Kelley was transferred to the hospital, where he was placed under the care of a team of doctors and medical specialists who had experience in treating radiation injuries. The initial prognosis was grim, given the massive dose of radiation Kelley had received. Radiation exposure at this level causes immediate damage to the body's cells, particularly those in the bone marrow, gastrointestinal tract, and central nervous system. The effects are both acute and devastating, leading to what is known as Acute Radiation Syndrome (ARS).

In the hours following the accident, Kelley's condition deteriorated rapidly. He experienced intense pain, vomiting, and diarrhea, as well as severe neurological symptoms, including confusion and disorientation. His white blood cell count plummeted, leaving him highly vulnerable to infections. Despite the best efforts of the medical team, it quickly became apparent that Kelley's injuries were too severe to survive. Just 35 hours after the accident, Kelley succumbed to the effects of radiation poisoning and died on December 31, 1958.

Kelley's death was a tragic loss, both personally for his family and colleagues and for the scientific community. His passing also underscored the extreme dangers of working with fissile materials and the potential consequences of even a momentary lapse in safety procedures.

Investigation and Analysis: Understanding the Cause of the Accident

In the wake of the Los Alamos Criticality Accident, a thorough investigation was launched to determine the exact cause of the incident and to identify any factors that may have contributed to the criticality event. The investigation was led by a team of experts in nuclear physics, chemistry, and safety, who were tasked with reconstructing the events leading up to the accident and analyzing the conditions under which the plutonium solution became critical.

The investigation revealed several key factors that contributed to the accident. First, it was determined that the plutonium concentration in the mixing tank had inadvertently reached a critical level due to an error in the preparation of the solution. This error may have been caused by a miscalculation or a mistake in the handling of the plutonium nitrate, leading to a higher concentration of fissile material than intended.

Second, the geometry of the mixing tank was identified as a critical factor in the accident. The tank's cylindrical shape and its reflective walls created conditions that were conducive to a criticality event. Specifically, the shape of the tank allowed for the formation of a critical mass of plutonium in a localized area, which then triggered the chain reaction. The investigation also noted that the presence of certain materials in the tank, such as water and the stainless-steel walls, acted as neutron reflectors, further increasing the likelihood of a criticality event.

Third, the investigation highlighted the role of procedural lapses and inadequate safety protocols in the accident. While the Los Alamos Scientific Laboratory had established safety procedures for handling fissile materials, it was found that these procedures were not always followed rigorously. In particular, there was a lack of adequate safeguards to prevent the accidental overconcentration of plutonium in the mixing tank. Additionally, the physical design of the laboratory and the layout of the equipment did not provide sufficient protection against criticality accidents.

Based on the findings of the investigation, several recommendations were made to prevent similar incidents in the future. These recommendations included the implementation of more stringent safety protocols for the handling and processing of fissile materials, the redesign of equipment to minimize the risk of criticality, and the introduction of more rigorous training programs for personnel working with nuclear materials.

Legacy and Impact on Nuclear Safety

The Los Alamos Criticality Accident had a profound impact on the field of nuclear safety, both within the United States and internationally. The incident served as a wake-up call to the nuclear research community about the potential dangers of criticality accidents and the need for heightened vigilance and safety measures in the handling of fissile materials.

One of the most significant outcomes of the accident was the development of improved criticality safety standards and practices. These standards, which were adopted by nuclear research facilities and laboratories around the world, focused on the prevention of accidental criticality events through better design, procedural controls, and training. The lessons learned from the Los Alamos incident were incorporated into safety guidelines issued by organizations such as the United States Department of Energy (DOE) and the International Atomic Energy Agency (IAEA).

In addition to changes in safety protocols, the Los Alamos Criticality Accident also led to increased awareness of the health risks associated with radiation exposure. The tragic death of Cecil Kelley and the severe injuries sustained by others in the incident underscored the importance of protecting workers from radiation hazards. This awareness contributed to the development of more comprehensive radiation protection programs, including the use of personal protective equipment, the establishment of radiation monitoring and emergency response procedures, and the implementation of medical surveillance programs for workers exposed to radiation.

The accident also had a lasting impact on the culture of safety at Los Alamos National Laboratory and other nuclear research institutions. The incident prompted a reevaluation of safety practices and a renewed commitment to fostering a safety-conscious work environment. This cultural shift emphasized the importance of safety as a core value in nuclear research and the need for continuous improvement in safety standards and practices.

Chapter 30: Rocky Flats Plant Incidents

The Rocky Flats Plant, located near Denver, Colorado, was one of the United States' most significant nuclear weapons production facilities during the Cold War. Operated by the Department of Energy (DOE), the plant played a crucial role in the production of plutonium triggers, or "pits," which are the core components of nuclear weapons. From its inception in the early 1950s until its closure in the late 1980s, the Rocky Flats Plant was at the forefront of the nation's nuclear weapons program. However, the plant's operations were marred by numerous safety violations, environmental contamination, and several serious incidents that have left a lasting legacy of environmental and public health concerns.

Establishment and Operations of the Rocky Flats Plant

The Rocky Flats Plant was established in 1951 as part of the United States' efforts to expand its nuclear arsenal in response to the Soviet Union's growing nuclear capabilities. The plant was strategically located in a relatively remote area northwest of Denver, Colorado, to minimize the risks associated with potential accidents or attacks. Operated by the Dow Chemical Company under contract with the Atomic Energy Commission (AEC), the plant's primary mission was to manufacture plutonium pits for nuclear weapons.

Plutonium pits are critical components of nuclear weapons, acting as the initiator of the nuclear chain reaction that results in a nuclear explosion. The production of these pits required the handling and processing of large quantities of plutonium, a highly toxic and radioactive material. The plant also handled other hazardous materials, including uranium, beryllium, and various chemicals used in the manufacturing process.

The operations at Rocky Flats were highly secretive, with much of the work carried out under tight security and with little public oversight. The plant employed thousands of workers, many of whom were involved in the direct handling of radioactive and hazardous materials. Over the decades, the Rocky Flats Plant produced tens of thousands of plutonium pits, contributing significantly to the United States' nuclear arsenal.

Environmental and Safety Concerns at Rocky Flats

From its earliest days, the Rocky Flats Plant was plagued by safety and environmental concerns. The production of plutonium pits involved numerous hazardous processes, including the machining of plutonium metal, chemical processing, and waste disposal. These activities generated significant amounts of radioactive and chemical waste, much of which was inadequately managed, leading to widespread contamination of the surrounding environment.

One of the most significant environmental concerns at Rocky Flats was the release of plutonium and other radioactive materials into the environment. Plutonium, in particular, is a highly toxic element with a half-life of 24,100 years, meaning it remains radioactive and dangerous for millennia. Even tiny amounts of plutonium can cause severe health effects, including cancer, if inhaled or ingested. Despite these dangers, the plant's operations resulted in the release of plutonium particles into the air, soil, and water around the facility.

The contamination of the environment was exacerbated by inadequate safety measures and frequent accidents. Throughout the plant's history, there were numerous incidents involving the release of radioactive materials, chemical spills, fires, and explosions. These incidents not only endangered the workers at the plant but also posed significant risks to the surrounding communities and the environment.

The 1957 Fire: A Major Incident at Rocky Flats

One of the most significant and well-documented incidents at the Rocky Flats Plant occurred on September 11, 1957. On that day, a fire broke out in one of the plant's plutonium-processing buildings, known as Building 71. The fire started in a glovebox, a sealed container used to handle radioactive materials, and quickly spread to other parts of the building.

The fire was fueled by plutonium metal, which is highly flammable when in certain forms, such as fine dust or shavings. As the fire raged, it caused the release of large amounts of radioactive plutonium particles into the air. The plant's ventilation system, which was supposed to filter out radioactive particles, was overwhelmed by the intensity of the fire, allowing significant amounts of plutonium to escape into the environment.

The fire burned for several hours before it was finally brought under control. By that time, it had caused extensive damage to the building and resulted in the contamination of large areas both inside and outside the plant. The exact amount of plutonium released during the fire has been a subject of controversy, but it is widely believed that the incident resulted in one of the largest releases of plutonium in U.S. history.

In the immediate aftermath of the fire, plant officials downplayed the incident, assuring the public that there was no significant danger. However, internal reports and later investigations revealed that the fire had caused widespread contamination and exposed workers and the surrounding community to significant levels of radiation. The long-term health effects of this exposure have been a major concern, with studies showing elevated rates of cancer and other illnesses among plant workers and residents of nearby communities.

The 1969 Fire: Another Catastrophic Incident

A little over a decade after the 1957 fire, the Rocky Flats Plant experienced another major incident. On May 11, 1969, a fire broke out in another plutonium-processing building, known as Building 776/777. This fire, like the one in 1957, started in a glovebox and quickly spread, igniting large quantities of plutonium and other materials.

The 1969 fire was even more serious than the earlier incident, as it threatened to cause a criticality event—a self-sustaining nuclear chain reaction that could result in a massive release of radiation. Fortunately, the fire was contained before it could reach critical mass, but it still caused extensive damage and resulted in the release of radioactive materials into the environment.

As with the 1957 fire, the 1969 fire led to significant contamination of the plant and surrounding areas. The building where the fire occurred was heavily contaminated with plutonium, and the cleanup efforts took years to complete. The fire also highlighted the ongoing safety issues at the plant, as it was later revealed that inadequate safety procedures and equipment had contributed to the severity of the incident.

The 1969 fire became a turning point for the Rocky Flats Plant, as it drew increased public and governmental scrutiny to the facility's operations. The incident led to several investigations and reports that criticized the plant's safety practices and raised concerns about the long-term environmental and health impacts of its activities.

Environmental Contamination: Air, Water, and Soil

In addition to the fires, the Rocky Flats Plant was responsible for widespread environmental contamination through the routine discharge of radioactive and hazardous materials. This contamination affected the air, water, and soil in the surrounding areas and has had long-lasting effects on the environment and public health.

- **Air Contamination:** One of the primary pathways for environmental contamination from Rocky Flats was the release of radioactive particles into the air. The plant's operations, including the machining of plutonium and the burning of contaminated materials, generated airborne particles that were released into the atmosphere. These particles, including plutonium and other radionuclides, were carried by the wind and deposited over a wide area, including nearby residential communities. Studies have shown that the air around Rocky Flats was contaminated with plutonium and other radioactive materials, posing a significant health risk to residents. The inhalation of plutonium particles is particularly dangerous, as they can lodge in the lungs and remain there for decades, increasing the risk of lung cancer and other illnesses.
- **Water Contamination:** The Rocky Flats Plant also contributed to the contamination of local water sources. The plant's operations generated large amounts of liquid waste, including radioactive and chemical contaminants, which were often discharged into nearby streams and ponds. These discharges led to the contamination of surface water and groundwater in the area, affecting both aquatic ecosystems and drinking water supplies. One of the most significant sources of water contamination was the plant's waste storage ponds, known as "solar evaporation ponds." These ponds were used to store liquid waste, including radioactive and chemical residues, until it could be treated or evaporated. However, the ponds were often poorly constructed and leaked contaminants into the surrounding soil and groundwater. This contamination eventually made its way into local streams,

affecting water quality and posing risks to public health.

- **Soil Contamination:** The soil around the Rocky Flats Plant was also heavily contaminated with plutonium and other hazardous materials. The release of radioactive particles into the air led to the deposition of these particles on the ground, where they remained for years. In addition, spills, leaks, and improper disposal of waste at the plant contributed to the contamination of the soil. The contamination of soil around Rocky Flats has had long-term consequences for the environment and public health. Plutonium and other radionuclides in the soil can remain radioactive for thousands of years, posing ongoing risks to anyone who comes into contact with the contaminated soil. The cleanup of contaminated soil has been a major challenge, requiring extensive and costly remediation efforts.

Worker Safety and Health Concerns

The Rocky Flats Plant was not only a source of environmental contamination but also posed significant health risks to the thousands of workers employed at the facility. The production of plutonium pits and the handling of radioactive materials exposed workers to hazardous conditions on a daily basis. Despite the dangers, safety measures at the plant were often inadequate, and many workers suffered from radiation exposure and other health issues as a result.

- **Radiation Exposure:** One of the primary health risks for workers at Rocky Flats was exposure to ionizing radiation, including alpha, beta, and gamma radiation emitted by radioactive materials. Workers handling plutonium, in particular, were at risk of inhaling or ingesting plutonium particles, which can cause serious health problems, including cancer. While some safety measures, such as protective clothing and ventilation systems, were in place, they were not always effective in preventing exposure. Over the years, numerous workers at Rocky Flats developed health problems related to radiation exposure, including various forms of cancer, respiratory diseases, and other conditions. Many of these workers were not initially aware of the risks they faced, as the dangers of radiation were not fully understood at the time, and information about the hazards was often kept secret.

- **Chemical Exposure:** In addition to radiation, workers at Rocky Flats were exposed to a variety of hazardous chemicals used in the production process. These chemicals included solvents, acids, and beryllium, a toxic metal used in the manufacturing of nuclear weapons. Exposure to these chemicals could cause a range of health problems, including respiratory issues, skin conditions, and neurological disorders. Beryllium exposure was a particular concern at Rocky Flats, as the metal is highly toxic and can cause a chronic lung disease known as chronic beryllium disease (CBD). Workers who inhaled beryllium dust or fumes were at risk of developing CBD, a debilitating condition that can lead to respiratory failure and death. Despite the known risks, beryllium safety measures were often inadequate, leading to widespread exposure among workers.

- **Occupational Safety Issues:** Beyond radiation and chemical exposure, the Rocky Flats Plant was also plagued by other occupational safety issues. The plant's operations involved heavy machinery, high temperatures, and hazardous materials, all of which posed risks to workers. Accidents, including fires, explosions, and chemical spills, were common, and many workers were injured or killed in these incidents. The plant's management was often criticized for prioritizing production over safety, leading to a culture where workers were encouraged to take risks and cut corners to meet production goals. This culture of risk-taking contributed to many of the safety incidents and accidents that occurred at the plant over the years.

Legal and Regulatory Actions

The numerous incidents and safety violations at the Rocky Flats Plant eventually led to increased scrutiny from regulators, lawmakers, and the public. Over the years, the plant was the subject of several investigations, lawsuits, and regulatory actions aimed at addressing the environmental contamination and health risks associated with its operations.

- **Federal Investigations:** One of the most significant developments occurred in the late 1980s when the FBI and the Environmental Protection Agency (EPA) launched a joint investigation into environmental crimes at Rocky Flats. The investigation, known as "Operation Desert Glow," focused on allegations that the plant's operators had illegally disposed of hazardous waste, falsified records, and violated environmental laws. In 1989, the FBI raided the Rocky Flats Plant, seizing documents and evidence related to the investigation. The raid marked the first time that a U.S. government facility involved in nuclear weapons production had been targeted in such a manner. The investigation revealed widespread environmental violations and safety issues at the plant, leading to a major scandal and increased public awareness of the dangers associated with the facility.

- **Lawsuits and Settlements:** The environmental contamination and health risks associated with Rocky Flats also led to numerous lawsuits from workers, residents, and environmental groups. Many of these lawsuits sought compensation for the health effects and property damage caused by the plant's operations. In 1996, a landmark settlement was reached in a class-action lawsuit filed by residents living near Rocky Flats. The settlement, known as the "Cook Settlement," provided $375 million in compensation to more than 12,000 property owners and residents affected by the contamination. The settlement also included provisions for environmental cleanup and monitoring of the affected areas.

- **Regulatory Actions:** In addition to legal actions, the Rocky Flats Plant was subject to increased regulation by federal and state agencies. The Department of Energy (DOE), which took over operations from the Atomic Energy Commission (AEC) in the 1970s, implemented new safety and environmental standards in response to the numerous incidents and violations at the plant. The EPA also played a significant role in regulating the plant, particularly in the areas of waste disposal and environmental contamination. The agency imposed stricter regulations on the disposal of radioactive and hazardous waste, and the plant was required to implement more robust safety measures to prevent future incidents.

Closure and Cleanup of Rocky Flats

The combination of public outrage, legal actions, and regulatory pressure eventually led to the closure of the Rocky Flats Plant in 1989. The decision to shut down the plant was driven by concerns over safety, environmental contamination, and the declining demand for nuclear weapons following the end of the Cold War.

The closure of Rocky Flats marked the beginning of a massive and complex cleanup effort that would take decades to complete. The goal of the cleanup was to remove or contain the radioactive and hazardous contamination that had accumulated over the plant's nearly 40 years of operation.

- **Cleanup Efforts:** The cleanup of Rocky Flats was one of the largest and most challenging environmental remediation projects in U.S. history. The site was divided into two main areas: the industrial area, where the plant's buildings and operations were located, and the buffer zone, which included the surrounding land that had been contaminated by airborne and waterborne pollutants. The cleanup involved the decontamination and demolition of more than 800 buildings, the removal of contaminated soil and waste, and the treatment of contaminated water. One of the most challenging aspects of the cleanup was dealing with the plutonium contamination, which required specialized techniques to safely remove and dispose of the highly radioactive material.
- **Waste Disposal:** The waste generated by the cleanup, including radioactive and hazardous materials, was transported to various disposal sites across the country. The most dangerous materials, including plutonium, were sent to secure storage facilities designed to isolate them from the environment for thousands of years. The cleanup of Rocky Flats was completed in 2005, at a cost of approximately $7 billion. While the site has been declared safe for limited use, including as a wildlife refuge, concerns remain about the long-term safety of the area, particularly in relation to residual plutonium contamination in the soil.

Legacy and Ongoing Controversies

The legacy of the Rocky Flats Plant continues to be a source of controversy and concern. While the cleanup was hailed as a success by some, others have criticized it as inadequate, arguing that significant risks remain. The site remains a focus of ongoing monitoring, research, and debate over the safety of the area and the health impacts on those who lived or worked near the plant.

- **Health Concerns:** One of the most contentious issues related to Rocky Flats is the long-term health effects on former workers and nearby residents. Studies have shown elevated rates of cancer and other illnesses among those exposed to contamination from the plant. However, proving a direct link between the plant's operations and specific health outcomes has been challenging, leading to ongoing debates and legal battles.
- **Environmental Concerns:** Environmentalists and some scientists continue to raise concerns about the safety of the Rocky Flats site, particularly in relation to the residual plutonium contamination. While the site is now a wildlife refuge, some experts argue that the risk of exposure to plutonium particles remains, especially if the soil is disturbed. These concerns have led to calls for further research and additional safety measures to protect the public and the environment.
- **Public Awareness and Education:** The Rocky Flats Plant has become a symbol of the dangers associated with nuclear weapons production and the environmental and health impacts of such activities. The site has been the subject of numerous books, documentaries, and public discussions, helping to raise awareness of the risks and challenges associated with the nuclear weapons industry. The Rocky Flats Plant's history serves as a stark reminder of the need for stringent safety and environmental standards in the handling of nuclear materials. It also highlights the long-term consequences of inadequate oversight and the importance of

transparency and accountability in government and industry.

Chapter 31: Sellafield Thorp Plant Leak

Sellafield, located on the northwest coast of England in Cumbria, is one of the most significant and historically important nuclear sites in the world. Originally constructed during World War II as a munitions factory, Sellafield was later repurposed for nuclear energy research and weapons production as part of the United Kingdom's growing nuclear program. Over the decades, Sellafield evolved into a massive complex encompassing various nuclear operations, including fuel reprocessing, waste management, and decommissioning.

The Thermal Oxide Reprocessing Plant (Thorp) was a central feature of Sellafield. Opened in 1994, Thorp was designed to reprocess spent nuclear fuel from reactors across the world, separating uranium and plutonium for reuse while reducing the volume of high-level radioactive waste. The Thorp plant quickly became an essential component of the global nuclear industry, handling fuel from countries such as Japan, Germany, and Switzerland. However, the plant was also the site of one of the most serious incidents in the history of the UK's nuclear industry: the Sellafield Thorp Plant Leak.

The Purpose and Operation of the Thorp Plant

The Thorp Plant was established as part of the United Kingdom's efforts to become a leader in nuclear fuel reprocessing. Reprocessing involves the chemical treatment of spent nuclear fuel to recover reusable fissile materials, such as uranium and plutonium, while isolating and reducing the volume of radioactive waste. This process is seen as a way to extend the life of nuclear fuel, reduce the need for fresh uranium mining, and manage nuclear waste more effectively.

Thorp's reprocessing operations were based on a complex series of chemical processes. Spent nuclear fuel, in the form of oxide fuel rods, was first dissolved in nitric acid. The resulting solution was then processed to separate the uranium and plutonium from the fission products and other radioactive materials. These recovered materials could be reused in the fabrication of new nuclear fuel, while the remaining high-level waste was vitrified and stored for eventual disposal.

Thorp was a massive facility, designed to handle up to 1,200 tons of spent fuel per year. Its construction and operation were hailed as a significant achievement in the nuclear industry, positioning the UK as a key player in the global market for nuclear fuel reprocessing. However, the complexity of the processes involved, combined with the inherent dangers of handling large quantities of radioactive materials, meant that Thorp also carried significant risks.

The Discovery of the Thorp Plant Leak

The Sellafield Thorp Plant Leak was discovered on April 19, 2005, when operators detected a significant loss of highly radioactive liquid within the plant. The leak occurred in the Feed Clarification Cell, a heavily shielded area where spent nuclear fuel is first dissolved in nitric acid as part of the reprocessing process.

The initial indication of a problem came when operators noticed that the level of liquid in one of the plant's containment vessels was dropping unexpectedly. This triggered an investigation, which revealed that a large quantity of radioactive liquor had escaped from the vessel and accumulated in the cell's secondary containment area. The leak was later determined to have been caused by a fractured pipe connected to the vessel, which had been leaking for several months before it was discovered.

By the time the leak was identified, an estimated 83,000 liters (approximately 22,000 gallons) of highly radioactive liquor had leaked into the secondary containment. This liquor contained a mixture of dissolved uranium, plutonium, and fission products, making it extremely hazardous. The accumulation of this material in the cell represented a serious safety and environmental risk, prompting an immediate shutdown of the Thorp Plant and a comprehensive investigation into the incident.

The Extent and Impact of the Leak

The scale of the leak at the Thorp Plant was one of the largest of its kind in the history of the nuclear industry. The 83,000 liters of leaked liquid contained approximately 160 kilograms of plutonium, a highly toxic and radiologically hazardous material. The leak also included large quantities of uranium and fission products, which are the radioactive isotopes produced by the fission of uranium and plutonium in a nuclear reactor.

The leaked material was contained within the cell's secondary containment system, preventing it from escaping into the environment. However, the sheer volume of the leak, combined with the high radioactivity of the material, posed significant challenges for cleanup and recovery. The incident also raised serious concerns about the integrity of the plant's systems and the adequacy of its safety procedures.

The impact of the leak extended beyond the immediate technical challenges of containment and cleanup. The incident resulted in the temporary shutdown of the Thorp Plant, disrupting its operations and leading to significant financial losses. The shutdown also had broader implications for the global nuclear fuel reprocessing market, as Thorp was one of the few facilities capable of handling spent fuel from a wide range of international customers.

Causes of the Leak: Technical and Operational Failures

The investigation into the Thorp Plant Leak revealed a series of technical and operational failures that contributed to the incident. One of the primary causes was the failure of the pipe in the Feed Clarification Cell. The pipe, which was used to transfer highly radioactive liquid, developed a fracture over time, leading to the gradual leak of material into the secondary containment area.

The fracture was attributed to a combination of factors, including corrosion, mechanical stress, and potentially flawed design. The corrosive nature of the nitric acid used in the reprocessing process made the pipe susceptible to degradation, especially in areas where it was exposed to high temperatures and pressures. Additionally, the pipe's design and materials may not have been adequately suited to withstand the harsh conditions within the cell.

Compounding the technical failure was a lack of effective monitoring and detection systems. The leak went undetected for several months, despite the presence of monitoring equipment designed to detect such anomalies. The investigation found that the plant's operators had failed to properly interpret the signals from the monitoring systems, leading to a delay in identifying and responding to the leak.

Operational practices at the Thorp Plant also came under scrutiny. The investigation highlighted deficiencies in the plant's maintenance procedures, staff training, and safety culture. There were indications that the plant's operators had become complacent about safety, relying too heavily on automated systems and failing to conduct regular, thorough inspections of critical equipment. This complacency was seen as a contributing factor to the incident, as it allowed the leak to persist undetected for an extended period.

The Response to the Leak: Containment and Cleanup

Once the leak was discovered, the immediate priority was to contain the radioactive material and prevent any further release. Fortunately, the leaked material was confined to the cell's secondary containment system, which was specifically designed to capture any leaks from the primary containment. However, the large volume of liquid and its high radioactivity made the cleanup process extremely challenging.

The first step in the response was to halt all operations in the affected area and isolate the leak. This involved shutting down the reprocessing process, draining the remaining liquid from the containment vessels, and securing the cell to prevent any further leaks. The plant's operators also began the process of removing the leaked material from the secondary containment, using specialized equipment to safely transfer it to secure storage.

The cleanup operation was a complex and time-consuming process, requiring the use of remote-controlled equipment and robots to safely handle the radioactive material. The high levels of radiation within the cell made it impossible for workers to enter the area, so all operations had to be conducted remotely. The cleanup was further complicated by the need to ensure that the material was safely stored and that no further contamination occurred.

The cleanup of the Thorp Plant Leak took several months to complete, during which time the plant remained shut down. The incident also prompted a comprehensive review of the plant's safety systems and operational procedures, with the goal of preventing a recurrence of such an incident in the future.

Regulatory and Legal Implications

The Sellafield Thorp Plant Leak had significant regulatory and legal implications for the UK nuclear industry. The incident was classified as a Level 3 event on the International Nuclear and Radiological Event

Scale (INES), indicating a serious incident with significant consequences. This classification placed the leak among the most severe nuclear incidents in the UK's history, drawing attention from regulators, policymakers, and the public.

The UK's Nuclear Installations Inspectorate (NII), the regulatory body responsible for overseeing nuclear safety, launched an investigation into the incident. The NII's investigation identified several regulatory failures and lapses in oversight that had contributed to the leak. The investigation found that the plant's operators had failed to maintain the equipment adequately, leading to the pipe failure. It also highlighted deficiencies in the plant's safety management systems and monitoring procedures.

As a result of the investigation, the NII imposed strict regulatory measures on Sellafield Ltd., the company responsible for operating the Thorp Plant. These measures included enhanced oversight, mandatory improvements to safety systems, and a requirement for more rigorous maintenance and inspection protocols. The NII also mandated a comprehensive review of the plant's operations to identify and address any other potential safety risks.

The incident also had legal implications, with potential liability for environmental damage and health risks associated with the leak. While the leaked material was contained within the plant and did not result in an offsite release, the incident raised concerns about the long-term safety of the Thorp Plant and the potential for future incidents. There were calls for greater transparency and accountability in the management of nuclear facilities, as well as demands for stricter regulations to prevent similar incidents.

Public and Environmental Concerns

The Sellafield Thorp Plant Leak sparked significant public and environmental concerns, both in the UK and internationally. The incident highlighted the inherent risks associated with nuclear fuel reprocessing and the potential consequences of failures in safety and monitoring systems. Public confidence in the safety of the Sellafield site, which had already been shaken by previous incidents, was further eroded by the leak.

Environmental groups and activists were particularly vocal in their criticism of the Thorp Plant and the broader nuclear industry. They argued that the incident underscored the dangers of nuclear reprocessing and the need for a transition away from nuclear energy towards safer and more sustainable alternatives. The leak was seen as a symptom of broader issues within the nuclear industry, including aging infrastructure, inadequate safety measures, and a lack of transparency.

There were also concerns about the potential environmental impact of the leak, particularly if any of the radioactive material had escaped from the containment systems. While the plant's operators and regulators maintained that the material had been fully contained, environmental groups called for independent monitoring and testing to verify these claims. The incident also led to renewed scrutiny of the long-term management of radioactive waste, with questions raised about the safety and security of storage and disposal practices.

The Future of the Thorp Plant and Nuclear Reprocessing

In the wake of the Sellafield Thorp Plant Leak, the future of the Thorp Plant and nuclear reprocessing in the UK came into question. The plant, which had been a cornerstone of the UK's nuclear strategy, was now viewed as a liability by some, with calls for its permanent closure. The incident also prompted a broader debate about the role of nuclear energy in the UK's energy mix and the viability of reprocessing as a long-term strategy for managing spent nuclear fuel.

Despite the challenges, the UK government and the nuclear industry remained committed to reprocessing as a key component of the country's nuclear program. The Thorp Plant was eventually restarted after the cleanup and safety improvements were completed, but its future remained uncertain. In 2018, the plant was permanently shut down after more than two decades of operation, marking the end of an era for nuclear reprocessing at Sellafield.

The legacy of the Sellafield Thorp Plant Leak continues to be felt in the ongoing discussions about nuclear safety, waste management, and the future of nuclear energy. The incident serves as a reminder of the complex and often precarious nature of nuclear operations, as well as the need for rigorous safety standards and robust regulatory oversight.

Chapter 32: Chalk River NRX Reactor Accident

The Chalk River Laboratories, located in Ontario, Canada, are among the most historically significant nuclear research facilities in the world. Established in the early 1940s as part of the joint British-Canadian nuclear research program during World War II, Chalk River played a critical role in the development of nuclear technology, both for military and civilian applications. The site was the birthplace of Canada's nuclear industry and has been home to numerous reactors, research projects, and groundbreaking discoveries in nuclear science.

One of the most important reactors at Chalk River was the NRX reactor, or National Research Experimental reactor. The NRX reactor, which began operation in 1947, was one of the most powerful and advanced research reactors of its time. It was designed to produce high neutron fluxes for a wide range of experiments, including materials testing, isotope production, and fundamental research in nuclear physics. The NRX reactor was a key facility for Canada's nuclear program and contributed significantly to the global understanding of nuclear fission and reactor technology.

However, on December 12, 1952, the NRX reactor was the site of a catastrophic accident that would become one of the earliest and most serious nuclear incidents in history. The Chalk River NRX Reactor Accident had far-reaching consequences for the nuclear industry, highlighting the dangers of nuclear power and leading to significant changes in reactor design, safety protocols, and emergency response procedures.

The NRX Reactor: Design and Operation

The NRX reactor was a heavy-water moderated, light-water cooled research reactor, with a design that was innovative for its time. The reactor used natural uranium as fuel, which was contained in vertical pressure tubes surrounded by heavy water (deuterium oxide) as a neutron moderator. The heavy water allowed the reactor to achieve high neutron fluxes, making it ideal for research purposes. The reactor was also equipped with numerous experimental facilities, including beam tubes and irradiation ports, allowing scientists to conduct a wide range of experiments.

The cooling system for the NRX reactor was based on light water, which circulated through the pressure tubes to remove heat generated by the fission process. The reactor core was housed within a large, heavily shielded containment structure, designed to protect operators and the environment from radiation. The NRX reactor was operated from a central control room, where operators could monitor and control the reactor's power levels, cooling systems, and safety mechanisms.

The NRX reactor was initially highly successful, providing a powerful tool for nuclear research and helping to establish Canada as a leader in the field. However, the complexity of the reactor's design, combined with the relatively limited experience of the operators, meant that the NRX reactor also carried significant risks. These risks became tragically apparent on December 12, 1952, when a combination of technical failures, human error, and procedural shortcomings led to one of the most severe nuclear accidents of the early atomic age.

The Events Leading to the Accident

The Chalk River NRX Reactor Accident was the result of a series of events and decisions that culminated in a catastrophic failure of the reactor's control systems. On the day of the accident, the NRX reactor was undergoing a routine series of tests and adjustments, which included the calibration of the reactor's control rods. The control rods, made of neutron-absorbing materials, were critical to maintaining the reactor's stability by controlling the rate of the nuclear fission reaction.

During the testing, one of the control rods became stuck in the partially withdrawn position, preventing it from being fully inserted back into the reactor core. This situation was already concerning, as the control rods were essential for shutting down the reactor in the event of an emergency. Despite this, the operators continued with the tests, believing that the stuck rod could be managed through alternative procedures.

At the same time, the reactor's cooling system was undergoing maintenance, which temporarily reduced the flow of cooling water to the core. The combination of the stuck control rod and reduced cooling created a highly unstable situation, with the reactor's power level increasing rapidly. The operators, realizing the danger, attempted to manually shut down the reactor by fully inserting the remaining control rods.

However, due to a series of communication failures and procedural errors, the operators were unable to effectively control the reactor. A crucial miscommunication occurred when an operator mistakenly gave a command to withdraw the control rods further, rather than insert them. This action exacerbated the already critical situation, causing the reactor's power level to spike uncontrollably.

The Reactor Explosion and Immediate Consequences

The rapid increase in power led to a catastrophic failure of the NRX reactor. Within seconds, the reactor core reached temperatures far beyond its design limits, causing the fuel elements to overheat and rupture. The extreme heat and pressure buildup within the core resulted in a steam explosion, which violently ruptured the reactor's containment structure and ejected highly radioactive materials into the surrounding environment.

The explosion was so powerful that it caused significant damage to the reactor building, blowing off the reactor's heavy concrete lid and releasing a cloud of radioactive steam and debris into the atmosphere. The force of the explosion also damaged the reactor's cooling system, leading to the release of large quantities of radioactive water into the reactor building and surrounding area.

The immediate aftermath of the explosion was chaotic, as operators and emergency personnel scrambled to assess the situation and prevent further escalation. The reactor was successfully shut down, but the damage had already been done. Radioactive contamination spread throughout the reactor building, and there were concerns that the reactor core could suffer further damage or even melt down if not properly cooled.

The Response and Cleanup Efforts

In the wake of the NRX reactor explosion, a massive emergency response and cleanup operation was launched. The Canadian government, along with experts from the United States and the United Kingdom, mobilized to contain the radioactive contamination and stabilize the reactor. The response involved hundreds of personnel, including scientists, engineers, and military units, who worked around the clock to secure the site and prevent further releases of radioactive material.

One of the most immediate challenges was to cool the damaged reactor core, which remained extremely hot and posed a risk of further explosions or a meltdown. Emergency cooling systems were hastily rigged up to flood the reactor core with water, reducing the temperature and preventing further damage. The highly radioactive water that had leaked from the reactor was contained and pumped out of the building, although this process led to significant contamination of the surrounding area.

The cleanup operation also involved the removal of the damaged fuel elements from the reactor core. This was a highly dangerous task, as the fuel elements were extremely radioactive and required careful handling to avoid further releases of radiation. Specialized remote-controlled equipment was used to extract the fuel elements and transfer them to secure storage. The entire process took several months to complete and involved extensive decontamination of the reactor building and surrounding area.

Despite the efforts to contain and clean up the site, the NRX reactor accident resulted in significant radioactive contamination. Large areas of the Chalk River site were contaminated with radioactive materials, including fission products, plutonium, and uranium. The cleanup operation reduced the immediate risk, but the long-term environmental impact of the accident remained a concern for many years.

The Human Impact: Radiation Exposure and Health Risks

The Chalk River NRX Reactor Accident exposed a large number of people to radiation, including the reactor operators, emergency responders, and cleanup personnel. The explosion and subsequent release of radioactive materials created a highly hazardous environment, with high levels of radiation in and around the reactor building.

Many of the individuals involved in the emergency response and cleanup were exposed to significant doses of radiation, particularly those who worked in close proximity to the damaged reactor core. The use of remote-controlled equipment and protective gear helped to reduce exposure, but the intensity of the radiation and the urgency of the situation meant that many workers received doses that were well above the established safety limits.

The long-term health effects of this radiation exposure were a major concern. While no immediate deaths were attributed to the accident, there were fears that those who had been exposed to high doses of radiation could suffer from an increased risk of cancer and other radiation-related illnesses. The Canadian government and the Atomic Energy of Canada Limited (AECL), which operated the Chalk River Laboratories, closely monitored the health of the exposed workers for many years, and several cases of cancer were reported among those involved in the cleanup operation.

The incident also had a psychological impact on the personnel involved. The stress and anxiety associated with working in such a hazardous environment, combined with the fear of long-term health effects, took a toll on many of the workers. The NRX reactor accident highlighted the human cost of nuclear accidents and underscored the importance of protecting workers and the public from radiation exposure.

The Investigation and Findings

In the aftermath of the Chalk River NRX Reactor Accident, a comprehensive investigation was launched to determine the causes of the incident and to identify lessons that could be applied to prevent future accidents. The investigation involved experts from Canada, the United States, and the United Kingdom, and it examined all aspects of the accident, from the technical failures that led to the explosion to the human and procedural errors that exacerbated the situation.

The investigation revealed several key factors that contributed to the accident. One of the primary causes was the failure of the reactor's control systems, particularly the stuck control rod, which prevented the reactor from being safely shut down. The investigation also identified deficiencies in the design of the reactor, including the vulnerability of the control rods and the cooling system to mechanical failure.

Human error played a significant role in the accident, particularly the miscommunication that led to the incorrect withdrawal of the control rods at a critical moment. The investigation found that the operators were not adequately trained to respond to the situation and that the procedures for managing such emergencies were insufficient. The lack of effective communication between the operators and the control room was also highlighted as a critical failure.

The investigation's findings led to significant changes in reactor design and operation, both at Chalk River and in the broader nuclear industry. One of the most important lessons learned was the need for redundant and fail-safe control systems that could automatically shut down a reactor in the event of a malfunction. The importance of thorough training and clear communication protocols for reactor operators was also emphasized.

The Impact on Nuclear Safety and Regulation

The Chalk River NRX Reactor Accident had a profound impact on nuclear safety and regulation, both in Canada and internationally. The incident was one of the first major nuclear accidents and served as a wake-up call to the risks associated with nuclear power. It highlighted the need for rigorous safety standards, robust emergency response plans, and continuous oversight of nuclear facilities.

In Canada, the accident led to a strengthening of nuclear safety regulations and the establishment of more stringent requirements for reactor design, operation, and maintenance. The Canadian government also increased its investment in nuclear safety research, leading to the development of new technologies and practices that improved the safety and reliability of nuclear reactors.

Internationally, the NRX reactor accident contributed to the growing recognition of the importance of nuclear safety and the need for international cooperation in addressing the risks of nuclear power. The lessons learned from the accident were shared with other countries, and they influenced the development of global nuclear safety standards and best practices.

The NRX reactor accident also had a lasting impact on public perception of nuclear power. The incident raised awareness of the potential dangers of nuclear energy and fueled public debate about the risks and benefits of nuclear technology. While the accident did not lead to a widespread abandonment of nuclear power, it did contribute to a more cautious and safety-conscious approach to nuclear energy in the years that followed.

Chapter 33: Kurchatov Institute Criticality Accident

The Kurchatov Institute, located in Moscow, Russia, is one of the most prominent nuclear research institutions in the world. Established in 1943 as the Laboratory No. 2, the institute played a pivotal role in the development of the Soviet Union's nuclear weapons program under the leadership of Igor Kurchatov, a physicist often referred to as the "father of the Soviet atomic bomb." The Kurchatov Institute was instrumental in the Soviet Union's successful detonation of its first atomic bomb in 1949, an event that marked the beginning of the nuclear arms race between the USSR and the United States.

Throughout the Cold War, the Kurchatov Institute continued to be at the forefront of nuclear research, contributing to both military and civilian nuclear technology. The institute's work encompassed a wide range of activities, including the development of nuclear reactors, research on nuclear fusion, and the study of radiation effects. However, the high-risk nature of nuclear research also meant that the institute was the site of several serious accidents, one of the most significant being the Kurchatov Institute Criticality Accident.

Understanding Criticality and Its Dangers

Before delving into the details of the Kurchatov Institute Criticality Accident, it is important to understand the concept of criticality in nuclear science. Criticality refers to the condition in which a nuclear chain reaction becomes self-sustaining. In a nuclear reactor, this is a controlled process, where the fission of atomic nuclei produces neutrons that cause further fission reactions, releasing energy in a steady and manageable manner.

However, if the reaction becomes uncontrolled, it can lead to what is known as a criticality accident. In such an event, the chain reaction escalates rapidly, releasing a sudden burst of energy and radiation. Criticality accidents are extremely dangerous, as they can cause severe radiation exposure, potentially leading to lethal doses of radiation for anyone nearby. The energy release can also generate intense heat, potentially damaging or destroying the containment structures.

The Context of the Kurchatov Institute Criticality Accident

The Kurchatov Institute Criticality Accident occurred on June 17, 1958, during an experiment involving the manipulation of a highly enriched uranium (HEU) assembly. The experiment was part of ongoing research to understand the behavior of nuclear materials under various conditions, and it was conducted in a special facility within the Kurchatov Institute that was designed for criticality experiments.

The purpose of the experiment was to approach the criticality of the uranium assembly in a controlled manner, using a variety of techniques to monitor and measure the neutron flux, the rate of fission reactions, and other critical parameters. Such experiments were essential for refining the designs of nuclear reactors and weapons, ensuring that they operated safely and effectively.

However, the experiment on that day would go tragically wrong, leading to one of the most severe criticality accidents in the history of the Soviet nuclear program. The incident not only highlighted the dangers inherent in nuclear research but also had lasting implications for the safety protocols and procedures at the Kurchatov Institute and other nuclear facilities worldwide.

The Incident: Sequence of Events Leading to Criticality

On the day of the accident, a team of scientists and technicians was working with a uranium assembly that was being brought to a near-critical state. The experiment involved the careful positioning of the uranium components, along with the insertion and withdrawal of control rods and other materials that affected the neutron economy of the assembly.

As the experiment progressed, the team monitored the neutron flux and other indicators to ensure that the assembly remained subcritical, meaning that the chain reaction would not become self-sustaining. However, due to a series of miscalculations and procedural errors, the assembly was brought closer to criticality than intended.

The exact sequence of events leading to the criticality accident is complex and was the subject of extensive investigation afterward. However, it is known that the accident was triggered when a critical mass of uranium was inadvertently assembled. This caused the neutron population within the assembly to increase rapidly, leading to a sudden and uncontrollable chain reaction.

Within milliseconds, the assembly went supercritical, releasing an intense burst of energy and radiation. The criticality excursion was brief but extremely powerful, producing a flash of blue light known as the Cherenkov radiation, which is characteristic of a sudden release of energy from a criticality event. The radiation dose received by those in the immediate vicinity was enormous, with some individuals exposed to lethal levels of radiation.

Immediate Consequences: Radiation Exposure and Health Impacts

The immediate aftermath of the Kurchatov Institute Criticality Accident was devastating. The scientists and technicians working near the uranium assembly were exposed to extremely high levels of ionizing radiation. The dose received by some of the individuals was in the range of several thousand rads, far exceeding the levels that the human body can withstand without suffering severe damage.

Several of the workers who were closest to the assembly suffered from acute radiation syndrome (ARS), a condition caused by the intense exposure to radiation. Symptoms of ARS include nausea, vomiting, diarrhea, and a sharp drop in the number of white blood cells, leading to a weakened immune system and increased vulnerability to infections. In severe cases, ARS can lead to multiple organ failure and death within days or weeks of exposure.

Tragically, some of the individuals exposed to the highest radiation doses succumbed to their injuries despite intensive medical efforts to save them. Others survived the initial acute phase but suffered long-term health effects, including an increased risk of cancer and other radiation-induced illnesses. The accident left a deep psychological impact on the survivors and the wider scientific community, as it underscored the lethal risks associated with criticality experiments.

The Response and Investigation

In the immediate aftermath of the accident, the Kurchatov Institute was placed under a state of emergency. The facility where the criticality accident occurred was sealed off, and a specialized team of radiation safety experts and medical personnel was brought in to assess the situation and provide care to the affected individuals.

The Soviet government quickly launched a thorough investigation to determine the causes of the accident and to identify measures that could prevent a recurrence. The investigation was conducted under strict secrecy, in keeping with the Soviet Union's policy of maintaining tight control over information related to its nuclear program.

The investigation revealed several critical failures that contributed to the accident. These included:

- **Inadequate Safety Protocols:** The safety procedures in place at the time of the accident were found to be insufficient for the type of experiment being conducted. There were no effective measures to prevent the assembly from reaching criticality, nor were there adequate monitoring systems to detect a criticality excursion before it occurred.
- **Human Error:** The investigation identified several errors made by the scientists and technicians involved in the experiment. These included miscalculations in the positioning of the uranium components and the failure to recognize the signs that the assembly was approaching criticality. Additionally, there was a lack of clear communication among the team members, which contributed to the confusion during the experiment.
- **Lack of Proper Training:** The investigation also pointed to deficiencies in the training of the personnel involved in the experiment. Many of the individuals lacked the necessary experience and knowledge to safely conduct criticality experiments, and there was insufficient oversight by more senior and experienced scientists.

The findings of the investigation led to a comprehensive review of the safety practices and procedures at the Kurchatov Institute. This review resulted in significant changes to the way criticality experiments were conducted, including the introduction of more rigorous safety protocols, enhanced training programs for personnel, and the development of advanced monitoring and control systems to prevent criticality accidents.

The Impact on Nuclear Research and Safety Culture

The Kurchatov Institute Criticality Accident had a profound impact on the culture of nuclear research, both within the Soviet Union and internationally. The accident served as a stark reminder of the dangers associated with nuclear research and the need for stringent safety measures to protect both the scientists conducting the experiments and the public at large.

One of the most significant outcomes of the accident was the strengthening of the safety culture within the Soviet nuclear research community. Prior to the accident, there had been a tendency to prioritize scientific progress and experimentation over safety concerns. The accident, however, demonstrated that such an approach was untenable, as the consequences of a criticality accident could be catastrophic.

In response to the accident, the Kurchatov Institute and other Soviet nuclear facilities implemented a range of safety enhancements. These included the establishment of stricter protocols for conducting experiments involving fissile materials, the introduction of more comprehensive training programs for nuclear scientists and technicians, and the development of more sophisticated instrumentation and control systems to monitor experiments in real time.

Internationally, the accident contributed to a growing awareness of the risks associated with criticality accidents and the need for global cooperation in improving nuclear safety. The lessons learned from the Kurchatov Institute Criticality Accident were shared with other countries, and they informed the development of international standards and guidelines for the safe conduct of nuclear research.

The Legacy of the Kurchatov Institute Criticality Accident

The Kurchatov Institute Criticality Accident remains one of the most significant and sobering events in the history of nuclear research. The accident not only resulted in tragic loss of life and long-term health consequences for those involved but also left a lasting legacy in the field of nuclear safety.

The changes implemented at the Kurchatov Institute in the wake of the accident helped to prevent similar incidents in the future and contributed to the development of a more robust safety culture within the Soviet nuclear research community. The accident also served as a catalyst for broader reforms in nuclear safety, both in the Soviet Union and internationally.

The lessons learned from the Kurchatov Institute Criticality Accident continue to resonate today, as they underscore the critical importance of safety in the pursuit of nuclear science. As the world continues to explore the potential of nuclear technology for energy production, medical applications, and scientific research, the legacy of the Kurchatov Institute Criticality Accident serves as a powerful reminder of the need for vigilance, discipline, and a relentless commitment to safety in all nuclear endeavors.

The Kurchatov Institute itself remains a leading center of nuclear research, with a continued focus on both fundamental science and the application of nuclear technology in a wide range of fields. While the memory of the criticality accident is a somber chapter in the institute's history, it has also been a driving force behind ongoing efforts to ensure that such an event never occurs again. The Kurchatov Institute Criticality Accident is a testament to the inherent risks of nuclear research, but it is also a story of resilience, learning, and the relentless pursuit of safety in the face of one of the most powerful forces in the universe.

Chapter 34: Soviet Submarine K-8 Reactor Accident

The Soviet submarine K-8 was a significant asset in the Soviet Navy's Northern Fleet during the height of the Cold War. Launched in 1959, the K-8 was a Project 627A "Kit" class (NATO reporting name: November-class) nuclear-powered attack submarine. This class was the Soviet Union's first series of nuclear-powered submarines, designed for both anti-ship and anti-submarine warfare. The K-8 represented a crucial step in the Soviet Union's efforts to match the United States in the nuclear naval arms race, providing the Soviet Navy with extended operational range, enhanced stealth capabilities, and the ability to deliver powerful nuclear strikes if necessary.

However, the K-8, like many early nuclear submarines, was a product of a period of rapid technological advancement where safety protocols and reactor reliability were still being refined. The pressures of the Cold War led to accelerated development and deployment of these submarines, sometimes at the expense of thorough testing and safety assurance. The K-8's tragic fate underscores the dangers inherent in operating nuclear-powered vessels, particularly in the harsh and unforgiving environments of the world's oceans.

The Mission and the Incident: Prelude to Disaster

In April 1970, the K-8 was participating in the "Okean-70" naval exercise, a massive display of Soviet naval power involving more than 200 ships, hundreds of aircraft, and tens of thousands of personnel. This exercise was designed to demonstrate the Soviet Union's ability to project naval power on a global scale, countering NATO's maritime dominance.

On April 8, 1970, while submerged in the Bay of Biscay, approximately 400 miles northwest of Spain, the K-8 experienced a catastrophic reactor accident. The submarine was cruising at a depth of about 160 meters when a fire broke out simultaneously in two compartments—Compartment 3 (electrical equipment) and Compartment 8 (aft torpedo room). The exact cause of the fire is not definitively known, but it is believed to have originated from a short circuit in the wiring of the submarine's hydraulic systems, which spread rapidly due to the presence of flammable materials and the confined spaces aboard the vessel.

As the fire raged, the K-8's crew faced a dire situation. The intense heat and smoke quickly filled the affected compartments, making them uninhabitable. The fire also caused a significant rise in temperature in the submarine's nuclear reactor compartments, threatening to escalate into a full-blown nuclear disaster. The situation was further complicated by the failure of the submarine's emergency cooling systems, which were unable to prevent the reactors from overheating.

The Struggle for Survival: Crew Response and Evacuation Efforts

The crew of the K-8, led by Captain Second Rank Vsevolod Borisovich Bessonov, acted swiftly to contain the fire and prevent the spread of the disaster. Bessonov ordered the submarine to surface, hoping that the fresh air would help ventilate the smoke-filled compartments and make firefighting efforts more effective. However, the fire had already caused significant damage to the submarine's electrical systems, making it difficult to control the vessel's operations.

As the situation worsened, Captain Bessonov ordered the reactors to be shut down manually. This was an extremely risky maneuver, as it involved entering the reactor compartments, which were now at dangerously high temperatures and filled with smoke. The crew members who undertook this task were exposed to high levels of radiation and extreme heat, but they succeeded in shutting down the reactors, preventing an immediate nuclear meltdown.

Despite the crew's heroic efforts, the fire continued to burn, and the submarine's condition deteriorated rapidly. The decision was made to evacuate non-essential personnel to the surface, where they were rescued by nearby Soviet ships participating in the exercise. However, a skeleton crew of 52 men, including Captain Bessonov, remained aboard the K-8 in an attempt to save the submarine and prevent it from sinking.

The Final Moments: The Sinking of the K-8

Over the next few days, the K-8 remained afloat, but its condition continued to worsen. The fire, combined with the damage to the submarine's systems, left it adrift and without power. The crew faced a desperate battle to keep the submarine afloat, pumping water out of the flooded compartments and trying to stabilize the vessel.

On April 12, 1970, after four days of relentless struggle, the situation became untenable. The fires had weakened the submarine's hull, and the flooding worsened. In a final, tragic twist, the towline that was being used by a Soviet rescue vessel to pull the K-8 to safety snapped due to the worsening weather conditions and the rough seas. With the loss of the towline, the submarine began to sink rapidly.

Captain Bessonov ordered the remaining crew to abandon ship, but the order came too late for many. The submarine sank quickly into the depths of the Bay of Biscay, taking 52 crew members, including Bessonov, with it. The K-8 settled at a depth of approximately 4,680 meters (15,354 feet) on the ocean floor, its nuclear reactors and torpedoes still onboard.

The Aftermath: Impact on Soviet Naval Operations and Nuclear Safety

The loss of the K-8 was a significant blow to the Soviet Navy and highlighted the inherent dangers of operating nuclear-powered submarines, particularly in the early years of nuclear propulsion technology. The incident led to a re-evaluation of safety protocols and emergency procedures aboard Soviet submarines. The Soviet Navy initiated a series of reforms aimed at improving the safety of its nuclear fleet, including enhanced fire detection and suppression systems, better training for reactor shutdown procedures, and stricter maintenance protocols.

The K-8 disaster also had implications for the broader Cold War context. It underscored the risks associated with the nuclear arms race, where both the United States and the Soviet Union were pushing the limits of technology to gain an edge in naval warfare. The incident served as a reminder of the potential for catastrophic accidents in an era where the threat of nuclear conflict loomed large.

The Soviet government kept the details of the K-8 incident shrouded in secrecy for many years, reflecting the broader policy of concealing information about military and nuclear accidents. It was not until after the end of the Cold War that more information about the incident became available, allowing for a fuller understanding of the tragedy and its consequences.

Environmental and Long-Term Concerns: The Sunken K-8 and Its Legacy

The sinking of the K-8 also raised significant environmental concerns, particularly regarding the potential for radioactive contamination from the submarine's nuclear reactors and torpedoes. The reactors contained highly enriched uranium, and the torpedoes were believed to be armed with nuclear warheads. The depth at which the submarine sank made any recovery efforts extremely challenging, if not impossible.

Over the years, there has been ongoing concern about the integrity of the K-8's hull and the potential for radioactive leakage into the ocean. Studies conducted by international marine research organizations have monitored the site for signs of contamination, but as of the latest reports, no significant radioactive leakage has been detected. However, the long-term environmental impact remains uncertain, as the degradation of the submarine's materials over time could eventually lead to the release of radioactive substances into the marine environment.

The K-8, along with other sunken nuclear submarines from both the Soviet Union and the United States, represents a lasting legacy of the Cold War era—a period when the pursuit of military superiority often came with significant risks to both human life and the environment. The incident serves as a stark reminder of the need for responsible stewardship of nuclear technology, particularly in the context of naval operations where the consequences of accidents can be profound and far-reaching.

Epilogue

As we reach the end of this journey through the world's most notorious nuclear incidents, we are left with a profound sense of both the potential and the peril that nuclear energy represents. The stories detailed in this book—each a sobering reminder of the fine line between progress and disaster—underscore a crucial lesson: the power of the atom is immense, and with it comes an equally immense responsibility.

The tragedies explored here are not just about radiation and fallout; they are about the human condition—our capacity for innovation, our thirst for power, and our struggle to control forces far greater than ourselves. From the cold winds of the Siberian taiga, where a nuclear submarine quietly succumbed to its fate, to the bustling streets of Hiroshima and Nagasaki, where the world first witnessed the unfathomable destruction of atomic bombs, these stories reveal the relentless pursuit of power and the often devastating costs of that pursuit.

Yet, amidst the devastation and the mistakes, there have been moments of heroism and resilience. Brave men and women have risked their lives to contain radiation leaks, decontaminate cities, and bring awareness to the long-term dangers of nuclear energy. Their sacrifices remind us that, despite the gravest of circumstances, humanity is capable of incredible courage and unity in the face of disaster.

As we look forward, the lessons learned from these nuclear tragedies should guide us in our approach to nuclear energy and technology. The risks associated with nuclear power—be it for energy production, medical advancements, or military use—are not to be underestimated. We must continually strive to enhance safety protocols, improve technological safeguards, and foster international cooperation to prevent future incidents. Transparency, education, and a commitment to rigorous standards are essential in ensuring that nuclear energy is harnessed safely and ethically.

The debate over nuclear power is far from settled. For some, it remains a necessary evil in the quest for clean energy in a world threatened by climate change. For others, it is a gamble too risky to take, given the potential for catastrophic accidents. What is clear is that we cannot afford to ignore the lessons of the past. As we advance further into the 21st century, the choice between harnessing nuclear power and managing its risks will become even more critical.

Ultimately, *Real Stories of Nuclear Tragedies* serves as a stark reminder of the dual-edged nature of human progress. Our ability to split the atom has granted us access to immense energy, but it has also reminded us of our vulnerabilities. In the balance of power and responsibility, we must tread carefully, ensuring that the pursuit of innovation does not come at the cost of humanity itself.

The road ahead is uncertain, but with reflection, learning, and vigilance, we can chart a course that respects both the power of the atom and the sanctity of life. The stories in this book are more than just history—they are warnings from the past, urging us to build a safer, more mindful future.

The End.